STRATEGIES

Of Entrepreneurial Leadership

Joshua Okello

Strategies

Of Entrepreneurial Leadership

Joshua Okello

Editors: Emily Puccini.
Ferdinand Ogumah

Joshua Okello
2014

First printing: 2014

ISBN 978-1-312-38982-3

Joshua Okello
80 Blythwood Road
Toronto, Ontario M4N 1A4

Dedication

To my brother Jared, family and friends who have supported me in my endeavours.

My sincere gratitude. Without your support and patience, I would never have achieved my dream.

CONTENTS

Acknowledgements

I would like to thank my editors Emily Puccini, Ferdinand Ogumah and Kristin Sawatzy, my fellow classmate Keith Brink, and my circle of friends, without whose help this book would never have been completed.

I also extend my sincere gratitude to my Entrepreneurship and New Venture Professor for supporting this project from the beginning and for allowing my team to use his tools to elucidate our points. Thank you for your patience and guidance.

I have to acknowledge the tremendous support of my family, my brothers Jared Okelo and Shem Okello. You are also my closest and best friends who never let me fall and if I do you still lift me up and put me back on track. May our almighty God bless you abundantly.

To my dear Chantelle, I am excited to walk this journey with you. Your encouragement, prayers and wise advice always sends me to pick up my pen and paper and write on topics that we both value and hold dear to our hearts: leadership and compassion. Your contribution to this book is highly appreciated.

To you, reader, who are holding this book at this moment, know that it was written for you. Were it not for you, I would not have wasted my time to put the gems in this book together in ink. It warms my heart to know that you are holding it now. All I can say is thank you so much for your support.

It is also important to mention the overwhelming love and support from my home church in Toronto. It has been a blessing to serve God's people in different capacities, and thank you so much for offering me these leadership roles. They were motivation towards the writing of this book. Peace be with you.

And to the names and friends that I did not mention individually, I pray that God will continue blessing you with wisdom to share with his children in different parts of the world where you serve. Let us make the most of the organizations, families and firms that we run. Continue inspiring future leaders. Tomorrows great entrepreneurial leaders are in the making today.

Preface

Back when I was a child, I was struck by how many false things I had believed, and how uncertain I was with the leadership structure and its beliefs. I realized that if I wanted to establish anything in the entrepreneurial field that was stable and likely to last, I needed to restructure my principles.

It looked like an uphill task. I decided to wait until I went to university to be sure that there was nothing to be gained from putting off this restructuring any longer. Year in and year out, I have been shifting the goal post until I picked up my pen and book and started journaling about the changes that I thought would be effective in the realm of entrepreneurial leadership. After setting all my worries aside, I decided to rearrange my life, locating clear stretches and attainable goals and objectives to which I was going to sincerely devote myself to without backing up, to ensure a complete overhaul of my former thoughts.

At that time I nullified all my false beliefs, after long introspection about what could be erroneous with our traditional leadership structure. To reconstruct a stable foundation, I relied heavily on scriptures, knowing that at least those meditations were indubitable. It was important that I define my foundational leadership philosophy. This is what helped me to define entrepreneurship as an attitude and approach that helps a person to take or make opportunities and to develop them further. Entrepreneurs never dance to the market tunes.

They create their own rhythm and get the market to nod to their beats; they go against the status quo promulgating their inventions with the hope of creating a useful product or service.

Growing up, we were told that children were our future leaders, and this is a statement I did not take for granted. In everything I did and still do, I look at my work from a leader's perspective. How are other people viewing me as a role model? Am I an agent of change? And exactly what change do people need? Leadership does not come on a silver platter, but it can be undertaken by anybody who looks for opportunity.

It was by answering these questions that I realized that leadership is a basic human need. Leadership is found everywhere and everybody qualifies to take on a leadership role. Is there anybody who can sit back and watch the basic unit of a society turn to ruins, when instead they can act and save the situation?

This book covers leadership in general, from family leadership to market leadership, as well as examining the traits and behaviours that are expected of leaders and entrepreneurs today. It is also important to highlight at this early stage that leadership has a lot of challenges and you must first formulate your own philosophy of leadership so that you can develop your own unique solutions to those predicaments.

Leadership is the key to success in any kind of organization. A leader should therefore be a planner, manager and above all God-fearing, as that is the foundation of wisdom. Think of organizations that have succeeded and some that have collapsed, and look at the root cause of their success or failures. A decent percentage of these successes or failures will originate within the organization's leadership, therefore leadership should not be undertaken lightly.

Joshua Okello

Introduction

Duo-contemplation is a word that I coined after being in strategic management for over two years. It is the ability to create two possible solutions in response to any unforeseen occurrences. Most entrepreneurs do not have this mentality and the single-focused planning makes it very hard for organizations to bounce back in the market in the event of any failures. Successful entrepreneurs never predict a single outcome and ride with it; they look at all possible choices and calculate tentative solutions for both. This elevates their management skills at all times, ensuring that they are prepared to deal with any difficulties that may arise.

Business challenges always come in pairs. They pose tough dilemmas to entrepreneurs and finding the best solution relies on the decision making ability of the entrepreneur in collaboration with his team of people who are all empowered with an in-depth knowledge that is needed to fully analyze the problem. But is decision making that important? Is there anything else that can help entrepreneurs in times of unexpected success and failures? When is the right time to suffer an opportunity cost? This book covers some of the basic yet complex ideas that most entrepreneurial leaders never choose at first sight when solving market challenges.

This book is also based on Christian principles and will show how they can be used to promote ethics and morals in a business setting. Is an action considered right just because the entrepreneur certifies it? Or is it because it is right that it is certified by the entrepreneur? We can call this *entrepreneurial Euthyphro's dilemma*. Can entrepreneurs pledge allegiance to higher forces than the bodies governing business markets?

Also covered in this book is business taxonomy, the *special specie* "entrepreneurs," and a description of who qualifies to be classified as one.

This book is based on primary and secondary research covering leadership and entrepreneurship. It not only shows that business is a fundamental factor to personal success, but is a basic need in our society today.

This book was written through interviews, online research, books, magazines, focus groups, articles, leadership and entrepreneurial experiences. Join me in embracing an exciting new philosophy of entrepreneurial leadership and discover how to prepare for challenges that come with the position in question.

Joshua Okello.

CHAPTER 1: LEADERSHIP

It is better to lead from behind and put others in front, especially when you celebrate victory when nice things occur. You take the front line when there is danger. Then people will appreciate your leadership
~ Nelson Mandela

The first responsibility of a leader is to define reality. The last is to say thank you. In between, the leader is a servant. ~Max Depree

Over the years, I have come to believe that, apart from God, business is the most important factor in our lives, especially in a globalizing world. As I started writing more and more on business, innovation and entrepreneurship, I came to learn that without good leadership there is no success. So, before a business is founded there must be someone in charge. Leadership therefore is the single most contributing factor to success in our communities.

- In a family set-up, there is always a breadwinner, who is most of the time the leader of the family. Children and other family members fully rely on this leader. These people need a leader who can provide, take care, protect, support, advise and be a role model. It does not matter whether you are from a single-parent or a two-parent family, you still need a leader. If you are that leader, then you must be ready and willing to meet the challenges
- Leadership is also needed in our faith-based organizations. There must be an individual who manages all the responsibilities and can be held accountable for all the successes and failures of the organization. (I am talking about

7

successes and failures because, most of the time, leaders' performances are measured as success and failure).

- Leadership is also needed in professional institutions and community centers. Someone must report the management, affairs and happenings in an institution to both the government and the public. They take part in overseeing the operations of different projects, and they also plan the future of the institutions in which they work.

- Politicians are leaders who engage in the daily affairs of a country. They manage the country's economy and hold jurisdiction to govern their nations and states. Political leaders are also often the heads of their countries' security.

- Businesses also need leadership. For success in any market, whether highly regulated or open, there needs to be a person with strong leadership skills. Somebody who is good with finance, who understands the market patterns, an organizer, a planner, a manager, most likely a people person. In general, we cannot live without leadership because leadership transforms chaos into order.

Now that we have briefly examined the importance of leadership, ask yourself: "what if I were the one in charge?" Some people do not consider themselves as leaders and often decline a position that puts them in the limelight. But can we really hide from leadership? Most people must be leaders in some area of life either leading an organization, a ministry, a community or a family. It is therefore better to familiarize yourself with leadership and be ready to be called upon at any time.

Throughout the Bible, God used people who were not considered "natural-born leaders". It is not wrong to think that you are not a leader, but if God has anointed you to become one, then you need to listen to His calling.

Think of Moses and how he was anointed. He was a man of no charisma, was not a thrilling speaker and he was the one whom God picked and used to lead His people. David was the last-born of Jesse, and we know in our societies today that last-borns are usually "the spoiled ones". This was probably true even in biblical times, yet David was the one whom God anointed. It is therefore good to understand that leaders are people who are anointed by God to fulfill a purpose and a need that is affecting his people.

What, then, is leadership? Here are a number of definitions of the word:

- The ability to give social aid to a mass of people who come together to achieve a common goal
- Doing the right things.
- Management and maintaining order in an organization
- The guidance and direction of a group of people
- The time when a person holds the position of a leader (according to the Merriam Webster Dictionary)

I would like to offer one more definition: leadership is laying yourself down for the sake of others. Not to say that the definitions above are wrong, but I like to take a different approach to and view of leadership. As a leader, are you prepared to lay yourself down for the people you are leading? Are you fully in charge of all situations and ready to be responsible for the best and the worst that your organization might encounter? Are you ready to stand up for your employees and be a voice for those who are in need? Are you ready to show love? A leader is a person who considers these questions and tries to live by standards that uplift the people he or she is leading.

As the Son of Man gave himself to be nailed on to the cross for the sake of the world, we should be in a position to stand firm for the people we represent. Some have called this type of leadership "servant leadership." In the history of the world, kings have ruled and reigned, judges have led and dominated, presidents have expressed and shown power in different ways but very few leaders have been there to lay themselves down for the sake of their people.

In the world today, we should be in a position to differentiate market celebrities and leaders. Most of the people we call business leaders are good examples of market celebrities; they exist to dominate without love, to promote themselves and to finish their rivals. Where is love? How are they laying themselves down for the sake of the common people?

It is good to understand that there are social leaders, spiritual leaders, business leaders, and relationship leaders, and this book will focus more on business leadership. However, other leaders can confidently borrow the strategies and practices described.

CHAPTER 2: LEADERSHIP AND INVESTMENT

"If you would be wealthy, think of saving as well as getting." ~ Benjamin Franklin

Do you know the only thing that gives me pleasure? It's to see my dividends coming in." ~ John D. Rockefeller

"A rich man is nothing but a poor man with money." ~ W. C. Fields

Some of the factors that determine our financial planning include age, personality, education, experience, health and family status. But what exactly does it take to build a financial empire? The simple key to investment success is strategic planning and discipline.

When Planning, One Needs to Think of Realistic Goals

Financial planning must have "short term", intermediate and "long term" goals. This is where you ask yourself why you want to be financially stable, and once that question is answered you can build a pyramid of plans for what to do with the invested money. It is always good to plan to spend, otherwise you will not be spending money to get money. This will not help you to achieve your organization's aims.

Reward Comes at Great Risk

All entrepreneurs know and believe that success is not for the faint of heart but for the bold who are willing to take the bull by its horns.

Business is about how well you can handle shock in the market and how you can cope with failures. People immediately think of financial risks associated with business but risks extend even to an entrepreneurs reputation. To paraphrase from Niccolo Machiavelli, "reputation must be guarded at all costs." Risk in business, according to my definition, will be any attempt that leads to the kind of disgrace that could precipitate a fall from power.

It is for this reason that most successful business gurus expand their portfolios. They tend not to rely on a single stream of cash flow but spread them across in a number of stocks from different companies. This is one way of reducing risk in the market but it does not completely eliminate risks.

Go for Value, Not Quantity

This is a great challenge to almost all consumers; often times we tend to skew our emotions and satisfaction towards financial abundance and forget about the value of the profit we receive. Let me give the example of a daily stock trader who makes decisions out of greed and egocentrism. His goal is to acquire numerous stocks at the end of the day, but real investors go for value; they know that investments pay better when accumulated over a lengthy period of time. Purchase stocks when they are low and sell them when they are high. This might even take more than ten years. Always remember never to trade stocks but to invest in companies. A trader is not highly engaged with the health of the business, all he thinks of getting his money and profits back, whereas an investor is interested in the wellbeing of the company.

Investment is a Philosophy, Study it

Investment philosophy is the critical study of the basic principles and concepts of appreciation in value and market knowledge, especially with a view to improving or reconstituting them. Investment therefore requires thorough research, study and planning. For startup businesses this process is covered in the business plan or in the marketing plans, either knowingly or unknowingly.

God First

Psalms 127:1 reads, "Unless the LORD builds the house, those who build it labor in vain. Unless the LORD watches over the city, the watchman stays awake in vain." It is easy to make our financial plans and work hard towards achieving our dream and forget about God in the equation. For a moral and ethical business, God plays a greater role in giving direction, including mandating a day of rest away from the busy work we do every week. Put God first, and start your financial plan today.

CHAPTER 3: PLANNED LEADERSHIP (AIM & SHOOT)

"Plans are only good intentions unless they immediately degenerate into hard work." ~ Peter Drucker

"Reduce your plan to writing. The moment you complete this, you will have definitely given concrete form to the intangible desire." ~ Napoleon Hill

A plan of any sort is an elaborate scheme or arrangement for a project's execution. To fail is to lack a plan. Leaders who do not do well mostly do not plan. Think of the leader of a successful company; reports to her board members, oversees the organization's operations, holds meetings with her managers, strategizes for the future and also takes care of her family. Without a plan, this leader is going to fail terribly. It takes a piece of paper and a pen to write a plan. As you read this, check if you have a piece of paper and a pen in your desk, pocket or bag. That is where planning starts.

One of my professors covered successful life planning in details. I would highly advise any business or organization that faces challenges to consider writing an "aim and shoot plan." Let us not confuse this with strategic planning. For more on strategic planning, check the chapter that follows. The type of planning covered in this chapter is a one-week plan. I will call it the "aim & shoot plan."

Aim & Shoot is a daily and weekly plan that divides portions of a project in fractions that can be worked on and achieved in a short

15

period of time. Someone once said, "Mile by mile it's a trial; yard by yard it's hard; but inch by inch it's a cinch." As the name suggests, aim and shoot is a plan wherein you set an objective and you hit it immediately. Hunters know that when they are in the field, they have to act one step at a time. Once they notice a target, they take aim and before the animal knows of their presence, they take the shot. That is what you need to do. Have daily and weekly aims and hit them before your time gets away from you.

Polar Opposition

Life is full of endless battles. We strive to excel, we want to beat our rivals in the market, we fight for our families, we fight for justice, we fight for human rights, we fight for better pay, we fight for promotions, and above all we fight to make it to heaven with Jesus someday. With all these fights comes opposition. If we give up and cave in to any opposition that we encounter, then we are going to lose. Failing to plan is a gateway to caving in before opposition.

The reason why we wake up early and go to bed late is because we want to face all challenges and be successful. The ability to encounter your challenges and stay on top is what I prefer to call polar opposition. There will always be polarity in the leadership scenario, therefore fight it back with a plan, repel it with a strategy.

Split Your Time.

Take each day of the week and split it in three: morning, afternoon and evening. You can find day planners cheaply in the stores these days. If you do not want to spend money on a planner, then just write your schedule down on a piece of paper. For those of us who like to preserve the environment, you can plan it on your phone, tablet, computer or most other electronic devices.

One of my best friends, an entrepreneur and a former classmate, once told me how he splits his time in portions of thirty minutes with five-minute breaks after every portion. The thirty minutes are for intense and rigorous work and the five minutes are for breaks, exercise, refreshment or relaxation. Find what works for you and divide your day in blocks of hours or minutes.

Top Five To-Do List

This is one of the best pieces of advice I have ever received. To work efficiently, you should never have more than five things to do in your daily list. Planning more than five is useless and discouraging. Remember that as an entrepreneur, there is no time to waste; you want to finish everything once and for all.

My personality results according to the Myers-Briggs personality test show that I am an Extroverted, Intuitive, Feeling and Perceiving (ENFP). This sometimes causes me to push my limits, and as a result I often wait until the last minute to accomplish tasks. However, after taking a business leadership and new ventures class, I trained myself to be on top of things and to avoid tight deadlines.

Dividing my day between fewer tasks makes it easier for me to follow my schedules and organize my daily goals. I encourage all readers who have not adopted these practices to try them, and if they yield good results then make them a routine.

17

Plan for Tomorrow Today

Take the last fifteen minutes of your day before you retire to bed to plan for the following day. When you wake up to a list of set objectives and with a plan in mind, you are reducing wasted time in the morning, boosting your efficiency and lowering your risk of burnout. Your mind works best in the morning, so do your best when fresh. Waking up to a plan gives you a rough structure for your day, making it easy to show up to meetings on time. They say the early bird catches the worm, therefore accomplish your errands as early as possible.

Have Time for Family and Friends

Were it not for the support of my friends, family and everybody in my contact list, I would not have been able to write this book, let alone run an organization. This is not an acknowledgement page, therefore let me go to the point. You need friends and family in life. Engage with people and learn from them. "Now the God of patience and consolation grant you to be likeminded one toward another according to Christ Jesus," (Romans 15:5 KJV). Be there for people who need you and they will be there for you too.

A family that prays together stays together. Be part of a family and enjoy the refreshing moments with your loved ones as you glorify Jesus' name.

CHAPTER 4: SOCRATIC LEADERSHIP

"Regard your name as the richest jewel you can possibly be possessed of – for credit is like fire; when once you have kindled it you may easily preserve it, but if you once extinguish it, you will find it an arduous task to rekindle it again. The way to gain a good reputation is to endeavor to be what you desire to appear." ~ Socrates

I do nothing but go about persuading you all, old and young alike, not to take thought for your persons or your properties, but and chiefly to care about the greatest improvement of the soul. I tell you that virtue is not given by money, but that from virtue comes money and every other good of man, public as well as private. This is my teaching, and if this is the doctrine which corrupts the youth, I am a mischievous person." ~ Socrates, quoted by Plato, 'The Death of Socrates'

Is there anything business leaders can learn from Socrates? Let us start by getting to know who this man was. Socrates was a classical Greek philosopher who is credited as one of the founders of Western philosophy. He came to fame through the writings of later classical thinkers such as Plato, Aristotle and Xenophon, most of whom were his students. He is widely known for his contribution to the field of ethics through arguments and self-defense that puzzled most of his antagonists.

As an entrepreneur and apologist, I know that business leaders can learn a lot from this great philosopher, from ethics and bargaining to intelligence and reasoning.

19

Piety

Socrates was so pious that he did nothing without the counsel of the gods, so just that he never did injury to any man. This dependence on God is what most entrepreneurs lack; let me call it *Socratic Proslogion* for now. The ability to have faith in God that all well-planned ideas can work is a trait that can propel any business to higher levels. Many entrepreneurs lose hope easily and shred their blueprints at early stages when they meet challenges. My advice is that you seek counsel from almighty God and he will bless you with faith and wisdom to believe that you can do it.

Temperate

Socrates never preferred pleasure to right. Accordingly, Socrates practiced temperance and self-denial to a degree that some thought ostentatious and affected. The ability to show moderation and self-restraint is very important when it comes to business. Successful entrepreneurs never work for money but to change the living standards of other people or to resolve a need. When you are starting a business, my advice is to never put money first; always think of your customers and the value that you are offering them. This is a concept that is very easily forgotten in business today. Any business that is focusing strictly on making money and nothing else is doomed to fail.

Intelligence

Socrates was so intelligent that he never erred in his judgment between what was good and what was evil. As a business leader, the ability to make right judgments is critical, especially in strategic management of any kind. One very successful investor once told me,

20

that it is never wrong to make mistakes if one learns from them. His second piece of advice to me was that it is okay to take risks, as long as they are thoroughly measured and well calculated.

Logical

Originating from the Greek word *logike*, the English term logic has more than one meaning. First, it describes the use of valid reasoning. Second, it is the study of reasoning. Socrates was a logician, who could reason out his thoughts in debates and arguments, and that is how he defeated most of the accusations against him. A business leader should be a person who can reason well and logically, and can tell when to quit if statistics do not tally in his favour. Business is about bringing value both to the customer and to the entrepreneur and if neither side is gaining, then it is time to apply *logike*.

Virtuous

Socrates lived a life of high moral standards. This could also be the reason why they teach business ethics in schools today. If something is not worth doing then do not do it. In my own practice, if something is against my moral and ethical standards, then however beneficial it is, I will not do it. Above all, seek wisdom from the source of all morality. Be pious.

Joshua Okello

CHAPTER 5: CONFRONTATIONAL LEADERSHIP

"Confrontation is not a dirty word. Sometimes it's the best kind of journalism as long as you don't confront people just for the sake of confrontation." ~ Don Hewitt.

"Direct confrontation, direct conversation is real respect. And it's amazing how many people get that." ~ Penn Jillete.

Confrontation is not to be confused with arrogance. What I mean by "confrontational" is the ability to directly oppose or challenge the action or authority of someone else. I also should make it clear to you that personality contributes a lot when it comes to being a confrontational leader.

Even though most entrepreneurs shy away from this type of leadership, it can benefit the organization if handled with care because it is different from arrogance. While arrogance demonstrates superiority and recklessness, confrontation sensibly questions the credibility of an action and how it is benefiting the entire organization.

In my daily life, I do not like confrontations of any kind but one of my business friends, a fellow school mate and an entrepreneur, once taught me that it is never wrong to question what is wrong. The only way to bring about change is to highlight what needs changing. This can look different and messy if you are in partnership or dealing with colleagues who are older, of higher rank, authoritative or intimidating.

23

According to moral ethics and expected office etiquette, no wrongdoing should be left unquestioned; otherwise the person seeing wrong take place will be equally responsible for it. However, if you are confronting, please make sure that you follow some basic principles:

Love

Your intention should be to correct the wrongs and the wrongdoer's understanding of the do's and don'ts of an organization. Before you speak you should remember Proverbs 15:1-2: "A gentle answer turns away wrath, but a harsh word stirs up anger. The tongue of the wise adorns knowledge but the mouth of the fool gushes folly."

Respect

It does not cost a penny to pay respect, however poor you may be. Know that you are dealing with a fellow human being, and do not put them on the spot so that they feel intimidated. Show respect and it will be shown back to you. It is a two-edged sword, and remember that what goes around comes right back around. When confronting someone, therefore, call them in private away from other employees and, with a lot of respect, show them where they have gone wrong. These Bible verses can help you correct with respect:

Matthew 18:15-17 "If your brother sins against you, go and tell him his fault, between you and him alone. If he listens to you, you have gained your brother. But if he does not listen, take one or two others along with you, that every charge may be established by the evidence of two or three witnesses. If he refuses to listen to them, tell it to the church. And if he refuses to listen even to the church, let him be to you as a gentile and a tax collector".

Galatians 6:1: "Brothers, if anyone is caught in any transgression, you who are spiritual should restore him in a spirit of gentleness. Keep watch on yourself, lest you too be tempted."

Consideration

Once a leader learns to regard the feelings and needs of others, he or she can address any issue in the organization with a lot of care and no problem need remain unsolved. Human beings are social animals and just like any other animals, both domesticated and undomesticated, if they are cornered and can sense danger, they will become defensive. Before they give in to power, they will always try to repel the attacks in any way possible, and this can cause damage to an organization. A considerate leader is an effective leader.

Wisdom

I am talking about spiritual wisdom, not simply experience or skills or any other forms of learned knowledge. Wisdom can only come from God, and a good leader is one who is anointed to serve with help from above. Simple courtesies, such as calling a person aside when you want to address a critical issue in a work environment, can make a potentially acrimonious situation into an opportunity for improvement. Seek wisdom from above.

Not all leaders need to be confrontational, but decide which style works for you and nurture it to serve you well. If you are going the confrontational way, then always remember not to cross the line between confrontation and arrogance.

CHAPTER 6: THE IMPORTANCE OF RUTHLESSNESS

"No person ever achieved success by waiting for someone to hand it to them. Successful people decide they want something and take action to get it. If you seek you will find. Get going. Now!" ~ Jerry Bruckner.

"Ask, and it will be given to you; seek, and you will find; knock, and it will be opened to you. For everyone who asks receives, and the one who seeks finds, and to the one who knocks it will be opened. ~ Matthew 7:7-8.

I once attended a focus group for our university on how to improve our business program. One topic that came up for discussion was marketing. The group included a number of alumni as well as first to fourth year students, and I was sitting as a graduand. One student raised his hand and talked about how ruthless my friend and I could get when it came to business.

I should make it clear that his definition of "ruthless" was to be proactive. It is true that my friend and I can be very proactive when it comes to meeting and engaging people in conversations. We always want to build our network and share what we are doing with people. This is what I prefer calling self-promotion.

When you are not recognized at an event where there are potential networks to connect with, it is upon you to get up and go meet people. Even though some people would be interested in talking to

27

you, they might prefer to sit down and wait rather than breaking the ice. As a business person, self-promotion is not only about giving away your business cards. I highly encourage taking a maximum of five business cards in a networking event.

Networking is not about distributing your business cards. It is about building your network and seeing how you can support other people and how they can be part of your company too. Business is a two-way street where you both take and give back. What you should always ask yourself is, "how can my business benefit the person I am engaging with?"

To know how you can partner and form organization synergy, ask relevant questions, get to know other business leaders, connect, and do not just connect with them because you want to add them in your business newsletter; go for their hearts.

Networking is like dating a new and beautiful girl you have just met. There are a thousand other men in the room, and how you present your self tells determines if you are going to walk away holding hands with her.

When networking, always remember that you are having a date with strangers, therefore professionalism is very important. Win people's hearts and if possible, go for their hearts and, if possible, win their minds as well. Let them walk out of that refreshment room wanting to talk more with you. Be charming, use hand gestures when discussing a topic you are passionate about. People will read whether you are genuine or not, so be yourself, have confidence, and never fake it until you make it, but rather faith it until you make it.

After the meeting, you always want to follow up with the people you met. This should not take more than forty-eight hours. Send them an email or give them a call if they gave you their contact information. Let them know how happy you are to have met them. Ask if there is any way your organization can help them and tell them how excited you are and that you are looking forward to knowing them better or working with them in the near future.

Even though this chapter is dubbed "The Importance of Ruthlessness," it should be named "The Importance of Being Proactive." If you have decided to take this approach, it will be good to have these ideas in mind:

Collaborations

The reason why you are looking for networks is because you want to build organization synergy. Building connections will take you far, and even if the people you meet do not connect with you to the point of collaborating with you, it is still imperative to realize that they have networks that might use your service or product. Be proactive in collaborations, and always think twice before you sign a business agreement.

A business or any leader should also draw ethical and moral lines that guide them in everything they do. One investor told me that some offers are not worth taking, especially if they go against your moral and ethical standards. So be keenly aware of the people you are talking to and let them know your beliefs before you partner with them.

Decision Making

The people you are going to meet will ask you tough questions and present you with dilemmas, and your ability to make a quick and precise decision is very important. Standing firm by your final answer and showing confidence will take you to a whole new level. To improve your decision making in matters relating to your organization, you should understand your business plan, your organization's missions and your vision. Think on your feet.

Clear Communication

As a business leader, it is important to communicate what is in your mind and make it crispy clear to people you are talking to. As you share about your company, always allow time for interactive segments as this will make people connect and understand more about your organization. Being unequivocal in your communication saves you a lot of time and reduces time spent responding to questions you have already addressed.

Speak for Others

Your business is not about you, it is about those who rely on it. As a business leader, you are communicating on behalf of your customers, your board members, your employees, your shareholders, your managers and other executives.

It is therefore advisable to communicate how your business is changing the world. People are always eager to hear new concepts and how they can be propelled further to support more people. You are the ambassador of your organization, therefore represent it well.

Talk of your successes; applaud your team even if they are not attending the event with you. Build enthusiasm that will trigger someone's attention to focus more on you. This is not the only book that talks about sharing a story. Tell a story, and again I say, tell a story. Stories are the best way to communicate your organization's missions to people.

Be Persuasive

It is not about convincing your audience that your organization or company is the best; persuade them to think like you. You want to make them see life challenges from your perspective and to do this, you cannot rely on convincing people. You can only convince people if they do not agree with your service, and this can only come after you have worked for them. Since this will not be the case when you first make a business contact, always persuade him or her to have the same mindset as you.

While persuading people, it is important to let them see how valuable your service is to them. How are they going to benefit from your organization? That should be your principle reason for networking.

.

31

CHAPTER 7: BUILDING A TEAM SYNERGY

"The strength of the team is each individual member. The strength of each member is the team."
~ Phil Jackson

"The greater the loyalty of a group toward the group, the greater is the motivation among the members to achieve the goals of the group, and the greater the probability that the group will achieve its goals."
~ Rensis Likert

A synergy is a systematic interaction of multiple elements that are more powerful together than they could be apart. Every leader dreams of bringing together a team that works in this way, but not many get the formula right. Building a synergy is like combining elements in a chemistry laboratory, where you note the risks and try to obtain the best end results. So what exactly does it take to build a team synergy?

Self-Evaluation

As a leader, the best thing to do for your organization is to first evaluate yourself, be honest with yourself and accept your weaknesses. We are not perfect. Even the most beautiful, when asked if they would change anything about their looks, they will identify a feature that they do not like in themselves.

Being honest with yourself and accepting your weaknesses and strengths is where success starts. The reason you start with introspection is because you want your team to compliment your strengths. Where you are weak, you find the right employee that can replace your weaknesses with amazing performance. After all, why would you hire someone with same qualities as you?

Never Hire a Résumé and Forget the Candidate

There are over 340,000 hits you can get if you type *job interview questions* on Google. Why bother wasting your time interviewing people who have studied all the questions and memorized possible solutions to your challenges? People who have sat in my interviews know and understand that I never ask ordinary interview questions. Job interviews are not high school enrollment questionnaires where you can cram the whole night and succeed in the morning.

As much as it is good to look at the résumé, that should not be the only or the main reason why you choose to hire someone. I have a high preference for hiring a high school graduate who is logical over a Ph.D. graduate who cannot think on his feet. I also understand that there are different personalities, and I factor it all in before I make a final decision. Some of us need time to contemplate, while others who are extroverts can constructively come up with an answer as they talk.

The success of your team and the power they unleash depends on who you hire, therefore take your time and get the right person. Most presidents who newly assume power are given 100 days to change the economy and revolutionize the government before the public begin to be disillusioned with them. This is not possible, as no economy in the entire world can change for the better in 100 days.

However, in small organizations, 100 days is enough for you to understand the strengths of your new recruit. Always give your new recruit at least the aforementioned number of days to keenly follow up with the quality of work that they do. These 100 days should also cover second chances, learning, correction, and teaching opportunities. Never fire any employee with the stroke of a pen. It is inhuman to do so. Let your employees know where they go wrong, correct them and give them second chances, talk to them, discuss your expectations with them and if they are not the right fit for the job then advise them to resign.

The team you build determines the magnitude of your organization's synergy. If an employee resigns from your company, call them a month later and ask them how they are doing. Show concern, and be willing and ready to teach them where they go wrong even if they no longer work in your company.

Display a Positive Image

As a leader, you are a man of the people! Groom yourself and build a positive self-image. As an entrepreneur, especially of a start-up, business meetings are not the same as sitting in a classroom lecture. Dress appropriately. The image you display will always give people an idea on how to classify you. If you are not running an entertainment or art business that requires you to dress casually, then avoid those jeans with holes on their knees and graphics all over them.

Work on your wardrobe and, if possible, have some dress pants, or trousers as some like to call them, repair your jackets or suits, get your shoes shining, and iron your shirts. Since you are looking for respect, authority and honour, maintain your appearance and set the image pace.

Personally, I am more confident when I am smartly dressed than when I am in casuals, therefore it is best for me to attend business meetings and go to work dressed up. Find some reasonable stores that offer quality products and invest in yourself. Be crispy clean.

Build Impeccable Character

Everybody is important. I am saying everybody because most entrepreneurs and leaders naturally rank people. God created us equal, therefore take your time and listen to people. Create time for people and people will create time for you.

Are you the type who never responds to phone calls? Texts? Emails? I highly recommend responding to people, even if it means informing them that you got their email and they should wait for your detailed response when you are free to send one. A lot of entrepreneurs wake up to a full inbox of emails, mail on their desks, text messages, and missed calls. Try your best to clear them out of your way, and remember that someone thought of you and spared their precious time to contact you. Show respect back.

If your team sees how committed you are to communication with all, they will be propelled to keep the standards and pace you set. At the least, respond to messages within forty-eight hours.

Use the Surrender Tactic

Self-defense is an innate attribute that comes as part of the human package. The ability to resist this strong urge to avenge yourself can propel your organization to higher levels. The ultimate goal is to build synergy, therefore never forget to surrender in heated debates. Get me right; always get guidance from the organization's core values. Now this is what I mean; if a customer calls you and they are not satisfied with the work you have done, you really do not have to be rude, however insulting they might be. "A gentle answer turns away wrath, but a harsh word stirs up anger." (Proverbs 15:1). Since you exist because of your customer, always remember to tone down your voice. It can also make your customers think that the mistake is mundane and you are committed to addressing it once and for all.

This lack of resistance disarms your opponent and keeps you at the fulcrum of the topic. Since you always want to swing and sway the discussions your way, it is better to keep calm. Share this with your team and let them serve your customers with respect and dignity. Your customers talk, and any little thing that turns them off can spread like a bush fire and ruin your business.

Value Your Team

If you keenly evaluated yourself as described in the first point of this chapter, then you probably realize that you are dealing with people with gifts that you are lacking. Nurture them. Your team holds the horsepower that propels the organization, therefore show them that they matter to the group.

Nothing motivates people like letting them know that they are valued. Maintain effective communication with them, and call them aside when something is wrong. Show them that you care, but do not pretend; show them that you *really* care. Lies can only go so far and they will all be unearthed. Value your team; they hold the potential of your organization.

Coach Your Team

If you cannot be a coach, or your organization cannot afford mentor programs for your employees, then advise your team members to find coaches in their lives. Let your team pick their idols and strive to imitate them. Remember that it all contributes to the synergy and conjoined success of your organization.

Coaches challenge, train and push people to do more than they think they can handle. That is what your organization needs for success. Successful leaders inspire and coach their team to go the extra mile. Show people the way and let them walk. As much as you are setting goals and targets for your team, they should set their own goals and break their own records. That is when your team enjoys being part of the organization. As a coach, train them to embrace healthy competition and to go the extra mile.

Have Faith

In a formal self-introduction that I gave to a fellow entrepreneur, I told him that my background extends to business administration-international development, philosophy and Christian apologetics. His question to me was, "why did you mix those contradicting things together? You must be a trouble-maker." In response, I paraphrased this verse: "But in your hearts honor Christ the lord as holy, always being prepared to make a defense to anyone who asks you for a reason for the hope that is in you; yet do it with gentleness and respect" (1 Peter 3:15 ESV).

It is not just about having faith that your business will do well, but about anchoring your faith in Christ and being ready to defend your beliefs. It can be great to have a team that shares common beliefs with you, but if you are not working with believers then use that opportunity to share the gospel with them. It propels your team to greater levels if you all believe in a common faith and the goals and expectations that come with that belief.

Build team synergy and catapult your organization to higher success.

Joshua Okello

CHAPTER 8: THE PARADIGM SHIFT

"Change will not come if we wait for some other person or some other time. We are the ones we've been waiting for. We are the change that we seek" ~ Barack Obama.

"Culture does not change because we desire to change it. Culture changes when the organization is transformed – the culture reflects the realities of people working together every day" ~ Frances Hesselbein.

"The world hates change, yet it is the only thing that has brought progress" ~ Charles Kettering.

Gone are the days when leaders used excessive powers, authoritarianism and cut-throat Machiavellian principles. In the old days, a leader was gaged as successful by looking at how many slaves he had, as well as how forceful and demanding he was. The more people you had following you, whether or not they respected you, the more you were considered an achiever. Inflicting fear in the hearts of your followers was deemed best when it came to gaining respect. What people did not comprehend was that fear and respect are two different things with different definitions.

Machiavelli highly believed that if you cannot be respected as a leader, the next best solution is to be feared without being loathed. This type of leadership cannot last. What if all leaders sought only to be

41

feared? There will be a lack of trust, no respect and no love at all between the leader and those he leads. A leader, although higher in rank, should lower himself to the level of his employees.

Historically, some leaders have lived by the maxim, "get others to do the work for you, but always take the credit". Nicola Tesla's alternating current system was credited to George Westinghouse, who funded Tesla's research, but not Tesla himself. Thomas Edison and George Westinghouse took glory for Tesla's exertion. Tesla languished in poverty, while Edison and Westinghouse made a fortune out of his efforts. Tesla was also the father of radio, but few people associate him with his achievements. From an ethical perspective, even putting aside my faith, it is wrong to do this. "A false balance is an abomination to the Lord, but just weight is his delight" (Proverbs 11:1).

"Get others to do the work for you, but always take the credit" is a misleading and a faulty principle. Your workers are not machines, and they deserve credit where appropriate. For a great leader who knows how to motivate, mentioning names and giving thanks and credit to your team is always very important. If a leader wins an award, that award belongs to the entire group, as everybody participated in the success that brought the award home.

The Paradigm Shift

To the ruthless, iron fist and authoritarian leaders, the ground beneath your feet has been shaken. The market has taken a different approach, and things have changed. Pride is a leader's guillotine. It is a noose that hangs all the leaders' ambitions. Scientific advancements and social science research show that human beings are more motivated when they are treated as part of an organization's success.

In the 18th century, Fredrick Taylor pioneered scientific management. This form of leadership focused on production by breaking projects down into tasks. Employees could then be trained to specialize in specific tasks. Taylor emphasized efficiency, control, and predictability. This view of leadership treated employees like instruments that leaders could manipulate. The focus of leadership was on the needs of the organization and not those of employees.

This scientific management of people, commonly referred to as *taylorism,* did not take into account the operations of the organization in its entirety. It treated people as robots or as a means to finish work, and did not consider the ethical side of dealing with employees. Great leaders should change from this perspective to a more inclusive way of dealing with people.

As the market changes focus from goods-producing firms to service rendering organizations, great business leaders have come to realize that employees need more inspiration than forcefully driving them to work. Great leaders share their thoughts and show concerns where necessary in order to support and advise their employees.

The traditional, top-down, ranked organizational management configuration is shifting. Leadership can be seen as vibrant and molten rather than static. It is an emergent property where a group of individuals bring their expertise together in pursuit of a shared goal. The emerging leadership paradigm exemplifies a leader as an individual who enthuses and empowers others with or without holding a prescribed position of power.

CHAPTER 9: FROM HOMO-SAPIENS TO HOMO-ECONOMICUS

"Waste no more time arguing about what a good man should be. Be one." ~ Marcus Aurelius

"Management is doing things right; leadership is doing the right things". ~ Peter Drucker, economist, management guru, author

"If your actions inspire others to dream more, learn more, do more and become more, you are a leader." ~ John Quincy Adams, 6th president

"The highest proof of virtue is to possess boundless power without abusing it."~ Lord Thomas Macaulay, British poet, historian, politician

Is it right to view human beings as assets? The answer could be both yes and no. If the former, then how do we need to translate the value of each and every person? If the latter, then how do we view human beings, especially employees? And what does economics say about the value and utility of a person? Is there scarcity in the number of performers out there?

The father of modern economics, Adam Smith, answered this dilemma in his book, *The Theory of Moral Sentiments*. Smith proposes the ability to form moral judgments, in spite of man's natural inclinations towards self-interest. He talks of the theory of sympathy, in which the act of observing others makes people aware of themselves and of the morality of their own behavior. Could he be talking about the "golden rule" in a way? Your guess is as good as mine.

Utility has been widely defined as the ability of a good or a service to satisfy human wants. Every entrepreneur's original goal is to induce effective change in his society. Often times, as entrepreneurs, we slip from this goal because of gains that come with innovations, and that is the foundation of treating employees not as human beings but as tools of gain.

Great leaders mark their boundaries and limits on how much they need to push employees to work. This can be practiced best when there are ethical standards in place. Ethics, from the Greek word "ethos" meaning "character", is the philosophy of systematically defending and recommending the moral do's and don'ts in a given situation. This concept is very crucial in the field of economics, wherein most entrepreneurs, innovators, managers, leaders, professionals and market controllers trade.

To understand this concept best, we need to know that morality and ethics go beyond subjective views of an individual. Two wrongs don't make a right, and whatever is wrong in a market place cannot be right anywhere else. Leaders should always be in a position to practice, goodness, fairness and justice. Greater productivity can result if employees feel loved and cared-for instead of being treated unfairly.

As leaders, we are responsible for the people we lead and therefore being just and treating employees with love can help us get to another level, not just as individuals but as organizations.

CHAPTER 10: HIRING A RÉSUMÉ AND FORGETTING THE CANDIDATE

"The best executive is the one who has sense enough to pick good men to do what he wants done, and self-restraint to keep from meddling with them while they do it."
~ Theodore Roosevelt

"Good management is the art of making problems so interesting and their solutions so constructive that everyone wants to get to work and deal with them."
~ Paul Hawken

"There is nothing so useless as doing efficiently that which should not be done at all."
~ Peter F. Drucker

It is a common phenomenon in the hiring process that a manager or a human resource professional hires a résumé instead of employing the candidate. This chapter is a guide to hiring etiquette, what to look for and what not to focus on. If followed keenly, proper hiring practices can result in productive operations for any company.

Administration and Organization

Most managers do not focus on potential employees' ability to multi-task while meeting tight deadlines and schedules. A track record of consistently committing and delivering is one sign of a high-performance employee.

Group Skills

No man is an island, therefore, looking for proven ability to work with other people is an asset when it comes to hiring. Strong team skills and understanding of group dynamics as well as competence in carrying out tasks in solitude is very important, but so is respect for differing personalities. You are looking for an employee who knows how to handle introverts and extroverts in a business setting.

Decision Making and Problem Solving

By presenting realistic job-related problems to a candidate, you can know how they think, reason, and how they would solve dilemmas that might arise in a workplace. It is handy to get examples of similar problems they've handled, and how they were solved. It is important to follow the cogency of their arguments and how they closely tie question to question.

Personality

As much as it is important to focus on the resume, it is also advisable to focus on personality, how the candidate responds to questions, gestures, and facial expressions and how confident they are and feel about themselves and their future job. As a president of an organization, my first challenge to people I interview is to ask them if they are smart. A lot of people find this intimidating; they lose their confidence, and push themselves into a defensive corner. Whoever

48

handles that question tactfully and satisfies me in all the above categories stands a high chance of getting the job.

Aptitude and Technicality

Always be on the lookout for an exceptional worker, a quick learner, a problem solver, and an influential person who understands technology and possesses impeccable communication skills. Ask your potential employee how she predicts the outcomes when solving a dilemma and how long it can take her to get to the solution.

Joshua Okello

CHAPTER 11: LEADERSHIP-MANAGEMENT DILEMMA (I)

"Great leaders are almost always great simplifiers, who can cut through argument, debate, and doubt to offer a solution everybody can understand." ~ General Colin Powell

"True leadership lies in guiding others to success. In ensuring that everyone is performing at their best, doing the work they are pledged to do and doing it well." ~ Bill Owens

Should a manager lead? Or should a leader manage? Leadership is one of the tightest ropes to walk in life, and the balance it requires is more than you can imagine. Most CEOs in organizations get mixed up in the myriads of roles that come with one title. This chapter is going to extract and analyze some of the dilemmas that most leaders encounter whether or not they are aware of it.

Power and Responsibility

Leadership automatically puts you in power, and most leaders find it a challenge to differentiate power from responsibility. This is where leaders start to use their responsibilities despotically, and the result is always a devastated team. A leader should know that he or she is in a delicate position, and that everything he or she does and says is being keenly monitored by those under him or her.

51

As a leader, you should learn your responsibilities before you exercise power over anybody. Know your limits, understand your people and know how much pressure you have to mount on your team; otherwise, you are bringing more harm than good to your team and to the organization.

Give Incentives

Every good worker deserves favour! Always reward your best performers and discipline your non-performers, but remember to do it with love. Give them second chances and be polite, especially when dealing with failures. It is not a must that the incentives be monetary; even thanking your team can mean much to them and can be a source of motivation to a lot of people.

Take your team out for lunch, order pizza online and celebrate victory, give your team a half-day break to show them that you are concerned with them and appreciate the quality of the work that they do.

Dealing with Failures

You have angry customers who are unsatisfied with the work your team has done. You have called your team into a board room and they can read tension on your face. Their hearts are racing and their faces show what they are thinking: "At the end of this meeting, one person must be fired!" Dealing with failures is more like giving incentives, only that instead of giving tangible rewards you are going to educate your team instead.

Please remember that people's abilities are not equal. Some are more gifted than others, and for them to make it to your company, they have shown some wisdom or strengths that you wanted to tap into. Therefore, avoid name calling and do not shout. Self-control is essential in this case. If someone fails, always remember to give them a second chance. Nothing is more inspiring than telling a failure that he or she can do better next time. Be ready to show them the way; that is why you are a leader and not just an employee.

You are handling someone else's future, therefore be cautious about what you say. Encourage them and never set your hands flying in disgust. Show love, motivate and encourage non-performers in your company, and if the same problem persists then shuffle your staff. Maybe the right people are in the wrong seats. Always remind them of their calling and educate them to be great performers.

Initiate Change From the Top-Down

It starts with you! As a leader, you should be a role model to people, not a scare-crow. Mind your language and treat people with respect. It does not cost a penny to pay respect, yet it rewards more than any revenue you can earn. Remember "The Golden Rule." In our Lord's prayer, there is a line that says "forgive us our debts, as we also have forgiven our debtors;" this should be a leader's prayer at all times. Learn to forgive, and change yourself before expecting that the team you are leading will change for the better. And always remember that "true transformation only comes from God" (unknown).

Joshua Okello

CHAPTER 12: LEADERSHIP-MANAGEMENT DILEMMA (II)

"You have touched on some good concepts here. Leaders must not just wield power, but place the bulk of the responsibility on themselves. While we need to share responsibility with our teams, the leader must shoulder the responsibility to ensure teams are provided with the information, tools, and guidance necessary to be successful. Individuals should be shown that their contributions are valued and learning from failure should be encouraged." ~ (*a comment on my blog post*).

Entrepreneurs are people who understand that there is little difference between obstacles and opportunities, and who are able to turn both to their advantage. This reveals strong leadership skills. As a leader, you want your name to be clean at all times and at all costs. Guarding your reputation builds your credibility and strengthens your business relationships; therefore remember that you are not only protecting your name but your brand as well. As a leader you should:

Build Alliances

Leadership and management of all kinds contain bits of politics. Politics has been defined as a dirty game, a game of numbers or a power struggle. To digress from these definitions, let us focus on business politics as a strategic move to form undefeatable alliances. Successful leaders talk to great people, men of wisdom, the experienced and people they regard as mentors. The first method for estimating the intelligence of a leader is to look at the people he has around him. In my previous chapters, I have mentioned the importance of having mentors and these are some of the simple actions that can propel you and your team to higher levels.

No politician governs alone and they will always merge into parties or bring parties together to form strong coalitions to defeat their rivals. As a leader, you gain a lot from forming coalitions with experienced people. It is all about learning, copying and advancing what other people have done. Yes, you might have great ideas, but you cannot stand alone. You need people, so take your time and listen to the person holding the lowest rank in your organization. They are also part of the alliance, and they might bring valuable information to you.

Be Ready to Serve

One of my best friends has served in the army. As a leader, he has been trained to serve those under him first. He puts them ahead of himself in everything, including simple things like serving meals. Since this has been part of him for so long, he now extends it involuntarily to everybody, everywhere he is. This is an excellent discipline in the forces and is something that leaders and managers should emulate. It illustrates the heart of servant-hood.

To those of us who are Christians, the Bible says, "each one of us should use whatever gift he has received to serve others, faithfully administering God's grace in its various forms" (1 Peter 4:10). It logically follows that if you are gifted in leadership, then you should use that gift to serve others. In a deductive argument, I would put it this way;

1. Leadership is a gift from God.
2. Leadership is one way of ministering God's grace to people

3. Serving others is a way of using our gifts for God's glory
4. Therefore, leaders can use their positions to glorify God through stewardship.

The world needs servant leaders, try and be one.

Take Risks

Entrepreneurs and leaders are known for their risk-taking capabilities. This readiness to expose themselves to danger, harm or loss is actually one of the most important characteristics of all business people. Since entrepreneurship is all about increasing your net present value (NPV), it is worth doing your calculations right before you try out a new idea. You must plan every step and act with boldness. This requires eliminating unnecessary risks in your business life. Risks, however, is nothing to fear when you are in business. More of this is covered in chapter twenty dealing with risks and uncertainties.

Mind the Two Extremes

As a leader, you should be both a manager and a friend. Never cross the boundaries and never offend the wrong person. You do not want to appear too bossy because then you will be scaring people away. As a manager, you want to build a harmonized team that brews the best chemistry at work.

As a leader, you should also be a friend to many. Your employees or people under your leadership should be in a position to see you as a man or a woman of wisdom from whom they can freely ask for help. Design an image that works for you and always let your people know that you are the leader. You definitely need respect from your team, therefore be willing to show respect to them, too. Respect and attention are two of the most affordable virtues; pay attention and attention will pay you back.

By this time, you probably understand that leadership challenges come in pairs and the decision you take is not important. What is important is living with the standards that come with the decision you make. What comes after the decision is what will determine whether or not you achieve your goals.

CHAPTER 13: LEADERS AND "ORGANIZATION CULTURE"

"A company can't buy true emotional commitment from managers no matter how much it's willing to spend; this is something too valuable to have a price tag. And yet a company can't afford not to have it." ~ Stan Slap

"The purpose of leadership is to change the world around you in the name of your values, so you can live those values more fully." ~ Stan Slap

"Engaging the hearts, minds, and hands of talent is the most sustainable source of competitive advantage." ~ Greg Harris

Off the top of my head, I can say with confidence that almost 75% of the organizations have "their way to do things." Any new employee who joins the company has to "do it our way." If you are reading this and your organization is not practising "do it our way," then you are destined for success. This is what I call organization culture. It causes more harm to you than good. So what exactly is organization culture?

Leadership

I discuss servant leadership in almost all of my literature, and this is not a new concept in the world of organizations. It is critical to mention that leadership is a title that requires management skills.

Management comes first, then the title follows. Impeccable management leads to excellent leadership. As a good leader/manager, you do not want your organization to become tangled in organization culture. Do all you can to stop this from happening.

Organization Culture

Culture is a behavior, a mentality and a philosophy that governs a particular group of people at a given time. This should not be misconstrued as an organization's goals, missions, and values. Organization culture can camouflage an organization's mission and vision easily, and make it appear that the organization is heading the right way. When work becomes a routine and not a natural passion that we have for constantly creating change and success, then the organization is gradually giving away to organization culture.

Managers can find it hard to realize that an organization is moving or has moved off track to develop organization culture. Even though culture also drives people to work, the presence of organization culture means that the enthusiasm that the team began with is ebbing away, and this can mean danger. Are your employees coming to work because they have to? Because they want to earn money? Because they want to please you? Because they have no choice, or because they are in love with the work they do? Organizations that have lost sight of their passion can be hard to change.

To maintain the original spirit without eliciting any fear, a leader should not be predictable. An organization that is willing and ready to grow should not be working the exact same way year in, year out.

Make changes, shuffle things around. It is also good to mention that these changes should not be so major that they take your organization a long time to adopt. It gets to a point when employees get used to communication, therefore avoid communicating the same way as much as possible. Show up when you are least expected, talk to employees, and ask them how you can help them improve their work.

When employees start asking you questions about how they should be working, it means that you are doing something wrong. Spending time with your employees removes barriers to flowing communication. Doing away with "organization culture" improves duo-contemplation. Since there is an expectation of change, your employees can easily adopt whatever comes their way. If a plan fails, it is never a big task to adjust to the changes that come along with that failure. This awareness is what you want as a leader.

Organization culture may drive people to work, but it is not an internal and natural drive that comes to a person when they are newly hired. As a result, old employees always give new employees time to burn out. "Let us give him two months, he will join the club. He will do it our way." This is first degree murder to employee motivation. Your organization is going nowhere with such talk. New employees are very observant, and sooner or later, they will "join the club." You have a philosophical-organization-slippery-slope where employees discourage one after the other. Organization culture can exist even if people do not talk about it.

An organization that has their chapel, or prayer meetings, or weekly round-table discussions every Tuesday can do it to a point

61

where it just becomes a routine and no longer furthers the goals of the organization. This is a risky place to be. Are your employees doing things because they are routine or because they want to grow? Create personal development opportunities for your employees so that your work place becomes a place of growth. Organization culture exists owing to lack of challenges.

Challenges

The human brain is the most versatile organ in the body. It is capable of changing the biggest dreams into reality. Think of all the great things that have been achieved by the help of the human mind. Planes flying through the skies above, people communicating on their cell phones, online commerce, electricity and light bulbs, geometry, locomotive engines and robots among others. When it comes to challenge, a leader should not challenge his or her employees but rather she should create an environment where her team sets their own goals and challenges themselves. This kind of organization is on the track to success. Your employees' actions extremely depend on you.

Enhance your organization's chemistry and let people do their best and beyond. To create a true synergy, people must be ready to work together, a pace that can only be set by the leader. With organisation culture, your work as a leader is effortless. Instead of interrogating your employees, engage them, use humor and let them enjoy their time in the office. Your employees have cozy homes where they can sit, relax and enjoy their time with family; making the office environment a work place for them prevents their mind from wandering away from the task at hand.

Organization culture kills the spirit at work. To easily identify it in your organization, invite guest speakers, auditors, volunteers and any other person who has some knowledge of what your organization is doing. Make them part of the team for at least one or two weeks, a month if possible. Sit with them and discuss what they saw happening in the organization. These should be people that you really trust with the organization's secrets, and they should be willing and ready to help you change for the better.

Remember that leadership is a title that comes from your management style. You can build your own style by learning as you go or by emulating great leaders whom you admire, but why reinvent the wheel if there are millions of ideas out there about how to address organization culture?

Joshua Okello

CHAPTER 14: LEADERSHIP CHALLENGES AND THEIR SOLUTIONS

"He who has never learned to obey cannot be a good commander." ~ Aristotle

"Leadership is lifting a person's vision to high sights, the raising of a person's performance to a higher standard, the building of a personality beyond its normal limitations." ~ Peter Drucker

"I have been impressed with the urgency of doing. Knowing is not enough; we must apply. Being willing is not enough; we must do." ~ Leonardo da Vinci

"Strive not to be a success, but rather to be of value." ~ Albert Einstein

"You miss 100% of the shots you don't take. ~ Wayne Gretzky

"Believe you can and you're halfway there". ~ Theodore Roosevelt

Welcome to Silicon Valley! This is where entrepreneurs, startups, and established businesses show their abilities to go against all the market odds to be on top. I presume that you are on this page, reading this book because either; a). You are a startup business person or an entrepreneur or b). You are running a stable business and would like to know more about business leadership. If the former, then you are in the right direction to make it to Silicon Valley, and if the latter, then you are in the chapter that will show you how to boost your revenues, net margins and efficiency.

As the founder and executive director of a registered international not-for-profit organization for over five years, I have encountered the normal business hurdles that every entrepreneur must meet, especially as a startup. This is also the stage where most entrepreneurs fold their tents, throw in the towel, give up or any other phrase you can think of that applies. Patience, they say, is a virtue, but you do not want to be overly patient when it comes to business. Stir up the waters, cause ripples, get to know your competitors, and always be ahead of them, but never be the first person to launch a new idea. As an entrepreneur, you have either met these challenges or you are yet to meet them and I hope this chapter will help you to navigate the ordinary challenges every business person must face.

Stay in the Acceleration Lane

Have you ever asked yourself why the acceleration lane joining a highway is long enough for you to reach a speed of over ninety kilometers per hour? This reduces the number of accidents and slowdowns that come with people joining a highway at a low speed. The same applies when you are starting a business; give yourself enough time to hit the maximum required speed. Most entrepreneurs think that they are going to make their first million immediately after they launch their business. I am not saying it is impracticable, but it is usually very hard to get to that level.

Therefore, make sure you have enough funds and resources to pull you through your first months if not years when you are starting.

Give yourself a minimum of six months without any income when you are a startup since nobody is going to buy your product or service the very first time you launch it. Never be discouraged. Keep holding tightly onto your budget until you start seeing the revenues, then hold even tighter.

Network

If you've been following my blog, podcasts and other writing I have done, you will realize that I talk a lot about networking. In the business world, you need people! Can you remember one of the five P's in your marketing mix? Yes, people! You need them. An old expression put it this way, "birds of the same feathers flock together". Network with like-minded people, listen carefully to advice they give you, involve them in your strategies, have a business mentor, ask questions and act on everything they say that you think can benefit your business.

Networking is not all about passing your business cards to people at a conference. In fact, if you are a day conference, my advice is to never talk to more than four people. Get to know the two or three to whom you are talking very well; build a connection or a bond. Let them know how your business can help them improve, show interest in their businesses and at the end of your conversation, give them your business cards. Email them in less than twenty-four hours and let them know how pleased and happy you are to have met them.

Be Part of Your Community

Did you know that there is a homeless program in your city? How about that youth rehabilitation center? Check out that church you walk by or that school your nephews go to for volunteer opportunities and you never know whom you will meet. It is also an easy way of connecting with potential customers and business contacts. As much as you want to get support from outside communities, always work at being accepted inside your own community first.

From a Big Heart

Business is about helping people. Use what God has blessed you with to support people who are in need. There are upcoming entrepreneurs who, like you, want to succeed in life. Support them. What goes around comes right back around. Be a mentor to young investors or those who aspire to be like you. Share ideas with them, including the ideas found in this book.

Prepare for Competition

My principle is, if you can't beat them, then plan to get them beaten. That might sound too ruthless, but this is what I mean: competition should not make you quit the game. Form partnerships, merge with your competitors, follow in their footsteps, and do what you do best.

Work with Social Media

Do you have Twitter, Facebook, Google+ and LinkedIn? If you do not use any of these networking sites, know that your potential customers do. Watch what you say on social media. Do not market there, but do engage people with your product or service. Be sensitive when you post content; never insult anybody, even if they attack you. So much depends on your reputation, so guard it as best you can.

Whatever you post on social media reflects who you are inside. Be nice to your followers and keep them engaged.

Speak at Events

Sign up for speaking events and practice your speaking skills. Not all entrepreneurs are eloquent orators, so do not stress if this does not come naturally to you. All you need to do is to train your brain muscle that you can do it. Take it as a challenge, find a place to practice speaking and share your ideas at least once a month. Once you are competent in it, speaking can become your strongest and cheapest marketing tool. Some people earn a living from speaking, and you can too.

Write

Nobody is born a writer, but you have been writing from kindergarten. You really do not have an excuse to say you cannot write. You do not have to write the wisest blogs or books. Just write! Writing this book was not a chore for me, because it was drawn largely from my personal experiences. You never know what will be helpful to your readers. . Write your story on how you see the world. Just practice until you nail it.

Never Give Up

They say go big or go home. But I say "go big or go bigger." Never lose hope when it comes to entrepreneurship, be creative and try new things. Some ideas might not work but if you keep trying, hopefully you will find the one that takes you to another level. It is just a matter of time. Embrace failure. It is not the end of the world. Always be ready to fail and pick yourself up when you do. Never give up!

CHAPTER 15: WHAT IS ENTREPRENEURSHIP?

"Every time you state what you want or believe, you're the first to hear it. It's a message to both you and others about what you think is possible. Don't put a ceiling on yourself." ~ Oprah Winfrey

"I have not failed. I've just found 10,000 ways that won't work." ~ Thomas Edison

"Success is walking from failure to failure with no loss of enthusiasm."~ Winston Churchill

"The price of success is hard work, dedication to the job at hand, and the determination that whether we win or lose, we have applied the best of ourselves to the task at hand."~ Vince Lombardi

Entrepreneurship is a structured procedure of identifying an idea, changing it into a business venture, sourcing its required resources and introducing it to the market with the aim of meeting human needs. Going by the definition itself, entrepreneurship is a step by step action; therefore, it requires a strategic plan.

Entrepreneurship might be a new word but the concept dates back to biblical times in the Old Testament. Commonly referred to as "trade" in the old days, it was an exchange of one commodity for another with the expectation of gaining value from what you trade. Today, we refer to value as profit.

71

Joshua Okello

Entrepreneurship has gone through radical changes throughout history. This metamorphosis has been catalyzed by civilization, inventions and innovations that change the world day by day.

For a start-up business to be successful, an entrepreneur should have a number of tools with him. Most of the great ideas that are working in the market system today are patented, consequently, making it difficult for one to use and/or claim ownership; however, you can come up with your own idea, patent it and get earnings and returns from it your entire life. This sounds easy, but business leaders need a lot of perseverance and determination. Focus is very important. What are some of the things that happen in the world of entrepreneurship?

Fifty percent of all start-ups die within the first year and almost ninety percent of all business fail after 10 years. Businesses of all types require regular enhancement in many areas simultaneously in order to be successful. Entrepreneurs should therefore embrace reasonable changes, admit their mistakes and aim higher. That is one means of becoming successful. Accept failures and move on.

CHAPTER 16: ENTREPRENEUR TAXONOMY

"Here's to the crazy ones. The misfits. The rebels. The troublemakers. The round pegs in the square holes. The ones who see things differently. They're not fond of rules. And they have no respect for the status quo. You can quote them, disagree with them, glorify or vilify them. About the only thing you can't do is ignore them. Because they change things. They push the human race forward. And while some may see them as the crazy ones, we see genius. Because the people who are crazy enough to think they can change the world, are the ones who do."

~ Apple Inc.

Taxonomy is the science of elucidating groups of biological organisms on the basis of shared characteristics and rendering nomenclature to those groups. In this chapter, I am going to classify entrepreneurs as a special group of the sub-species *homo sapiens sapiens.* This is not to say that entrepreneurs are of a different biological species from any other human being, but they hold distinctive characteristics that set them apart from all else. Since there are no definitive features to qualify them as species of their own, this qualifies everybody to be a potential entrepreneur; but some people stand out because of their resilience and persistence.

Some have called them eccentric; they are always in their own world, they like to cause chaos, they can be authoritative, and they never give up. Entrepreneurs like to go against the currents and are great risk takers. They have faith in their efforts, but plan before they

73

leap. Strategy is always their main tool. They slip, but they never fall; even if they fail in a particular area, they understand that failure is a part of success. Some of the unusual traits that most entrepreneurs have in common include:

Disrespect to the Status Quo

Entrepreneurs delete "status quo" from their dictionaries. They always go against the currents, and nothing can stop them from pursuing their vision. Once they make up their minds to achieve something, they will attempt it even if there are formidable barriers in their way. The choice of starting a business in itself defies statistics. Entrepreneurs who are value driven tend to perform better than the profit driven.

Tenacity

This is the ability to grip something firmly for a prolonged period of time before you let it go. Entrepreneurs will work with an idea for a long time before they let it slip from their hands. For the most part, they are not worried about the time it takes before they see their dreams come true. Tenacity drives them in tough economic times, and since they understand sinusoidal market behavior, they anticipate light at the end of the tunnel.

Self Belief

As the name suggests, to be an entrepreneur you must have self-confidence and believe in yourself before anybody else believes in you.

"Whatever the mind of man can conceive and believe, it can achieve" (Napoleon Hill). Most entrepreneurs believe in themselves and their potential. After all, it is never wrong to try, if you are trying the idea that will succeed. "It is only when you hitch yourself to something greater than you that you realize your true potentials" (Barack Obama).

Duo-Contemplation

Duo-contemplation is a word that I coined after being in strategic management for over two years. It is the ability to model a new strategy to use in preparation to any unforeseen occurrences. Most entrepreneurs do not have this mentality and the single line of thought makes it very hard for organizations to bounce back in the market in case of any unpredicted outcome. Successful entrepreneurs never take one train of thought and ride it; they look at all possibilities and calculate a tentative solution for each. This elevates their management skills at all times.

Design a Master Piece

Leonardo da Vinci is crowned for his masterpiece *Mona Lisa;* Michelangelo, contender for the title of the archetypal Renaissance man, is known for his masterpiece *Pieta*. In more recent years, Martin Luther King Jr. was known for his phrase "I have a dream," Barack Obama was propelled to the presidency of the United States of America by the three words "yes we can." These are masterpieces that were crafted by the artists themselves. Successful entrepreneurs also develop masterpieces, things that make them standout and unique. These are also ideas that, later on in history, are considered to have revolutionized an age. As an entrepreneur, you should develop your own masterpiece.

Entrepreneurs are few in numbers, but through technological advancements and a paradigm shift that has taken place in the global workforce, there has been a rise in the number of people who start their own businesses. My question to you is: do you fall under the classification of an entrepreneur? Yes you do!

CHAPTER 17: BUSINESS BELIEFS, KNOWLEDGE & PHILOSOPHY

"Without deviation from the norm, progress is not possible." ~ Frank Zappa

"Do not fear to be eccentric in opinion, for every opinion now accepted was once eccentric." ~ Bertrand Russell

Episentreology- this word has its roots in Greek and English, derived from three common and popular words: the Greek words *episteme-*and *ology*, and the English word *entrepreneurship*. E*pisteme* means knowledge, entrepreneurship means organizing and operating a business and *ology-*means study. *Episentreology,* therefore, is the study and understanding of the knowledge of organizing and operating a business. Not only is this a new word, but the study of understanding the knowledge behind business ideas is a new concept. In this chapter, we are going to visualize beyond the structure of a business to understanding its true worth. As you read along, ask yourself: are some markets overpriced, overvalued, undervalued, or underpriced? What exactly is business knowledge?

This part of the book also looks at business from a philosophical point of view by engaging ideas from some of history's best-known philosophers. *Episentreology* is the study and understanding of the philosophy of business. It questions what business knowledge is and how it can be acquired, and the extent to which business knowledge must be elucidated to gain excellent results. Business knowledge is

77

therefore a belief that is held by particular people who are interested in seeing better results through investments.

The next question we are going to ask ourselves is, "does everybody on planet earth have the potential of being successful in business?" Before we try to answer this, it would be better to first understand that *episentreology* is something that has existed since the advent of civilization.

Business is a discipline that has come to affect almost everything we see in the world today. Churches are operated according to principles of both spirituality and business. They file their taxes, keep all their financial books, have managers, directors and other governing bodies. Even if you are operating and running a ministry or a social work project, at some point you will encounter business in life. Business is one unavoidable thing that keeps the world going.

Families today operate as businesses. In every family, there is at least one person who is in charge of purchases, another one in charge of finances, another one in charge of the daily operations and management of a family. It is all business. Is it wrong to operate a family as a business? Whatever answer we pick, either yes or no, the truth is, there will still be the business element to be dealt with.

Instead of reviewing basic business philosophy and speaking in jargon, I am going to simply describe business as the trade of services or goods for a standard means of payment that offers value to both the buyer and the seller. As a family, have you bought anything in the market this week? If yes, you used *episentreology*. The ability to ask the utility of a substance relative to the value exchanged for it reveals our inherent understanding of business knowledge in this case.

Everybody has some business knowledge, even though they may deny it. I always ask students why they are not studying business and the response I get is the same. "Business has got a lot of math in it". What I find ironic about this ideology is that most university students must learn statistics, which is just as complex as business math. *Episentreology* is not limited to understanding the mathematical side of entrepreneurship. However, it can be beneficial to understand this side too, especially finance and accounting. How do People Acquire *Episentreology?*

Scarcity of Resources.

Economics is a branch of the social sciences that studies the behavior of groups of people and how they create utility out of scarce resources. Because of scarcity, human beings have practiced what I call *maximizing utility of resources*. The push towards maximizing the utility or the usefulness of a resource makes people develop in-depth knowledge of that resource's increasing value.

Scarcity of resources is enough in itself to make people acquire business knowledge.

Economy.

Although most of the time, the economy is in an upward trajectory, most entrepreneurs and business people know that it is also a cyclical trajectory, marked by peaks and valleys. Because of this unstable economic growth, people tend to learn from their mistakes and develop a system that helps them understand the business life in relation to the economy. Inflation and deflation can help people gain more business truths and knowledge.

Inflation is always marked by fluctuation; public purchasing power drops and the prices of goods and services skyrocket. During these times, buyers find it very hard as life gets expensive and the value they get for their dollars spent is decreased. The economy acts as one catalyst of *episentreology*.

History
George Orwell once said, "The most effective way to destroy people is to deny and obliterate their own understanding of their history."

The 1997 economic crush spread spasmodically to different continents, putting the global markets at greater risks. Its ripple effects were felt in the U.S. economy in 1998, crushing all of the America's economic developments and financial growth since the last financial crisis of the 1930s.

Human beings have learned from the past, and because of this, there has been a trend to make the world a better place. During such financial crises, people tend to spend less, hence there is a natural reaction to the market that is directly proportional to the recession rate.

The memory of historic depressions causes people to spend wisely, offering a learning opportunity for the benefit of people at present. The history of economics expounds in details how people learn and adopt better ways of operating businesses that support healthy economies.

Schools of Thought

Paradigm shifts always offer a dichotomy between the old and the new. Many people in entrepreneurship and leadership hold a common opinion and philosophy about the market. These particular economic and leadership schools of thought have trained people to acquire more business knowledge and understanding of market principles.

People who hold these mindsets establish them as core market beliefs that guide them in operating and running their businesses. Since the economic future is usually predictable, there is a strive towards excellence; and this is the type of mindset that great leaders and entrepreneurs should adopt. *Episentreology* has educated people to master some of the basic principles behind investments, either knowingly or knowingly.

81

Joshua Okello

CHAPTER 18: FOUNDATIONS OF ENTREPRENEURIAL SUCCESS.

"In order to succeed, your desire for success should be greater than your fear of failure." ~ Bill Cosby.

"Success consists of going from failure to failure without loss of enthusiasm." ~ Winston Churchill.

"Coming together is a beginning, keeping together is a progress; working together is success." ~ Henry Ford.

Business Formula

Entrepreneurship is not embedded in our genetics, but it can be learned. Even if you do not study business, through practice you will come to grasp the flow, make it part of you and start looking at things in terms of value. Human beings have got an ingrained business formula in them that, when exercised, can lead to success in revenue generation.

Even if an entrepreneur was to go to school to study entrepreneurship, it gets to a point where you have to stop learning and get to work. Business is like a language; you can only learn it by practicing it. Good entrepreneurs grasp this concept at an early stage, but this does not mean that they never make errors in judgment.

In the previous chapter, I stated that everybody has got business knowledge, therefore what entrepreneurs need to do is to exercise their

83

business muscles. Understanding market environments, when to invest and when to pull out is critical.

However, it is also wise not to be greedy in business. Always think of others, including your competitors, and love them as you love your customers. Business is not a one person game; it requires a collection of ideas for it to be productive. These people are known as stakeholders. Take care of your stakeholders and let the business grow by itself.

People of Influence

As an entrepreneur, you should be a person of influence. Build a name and let people know you for what you do best. Preserve it, maintain it and build a close attachment to it. People will be inspired by just looking at how passionate you are about what you are doing. All great ideas start from just one person, and then it spreads little by little until you get a mass of people following you. As an entrepreneur, you should build a cult-like following.

Good examples of this are the technology gurus. Facebook has become a household name in every family; Google is on almost everybody's mind, Microsoft as well. These are companies that breed a cult-like following. It is not a must that you have millions of followers for success, but your idea or your innovation should be very easy to connect with.

To be an influential leader, you should be ready to nurture and mentor other people. Always create time for ambitious people behind you; be encouraging, offer advice and support to them. No man is an island, therefore we need each other. It is also important to notice that mentorship programs are symbiotically beneficial. Much can be learned and gained through the exchange of ideas, you gain and learn a lot, not only about people, but about how to make your organization better. To be influential, you should be in a position to appreciate other people's efforts to greatness. Be positive and give directions to success.

Self-Awareness

It all starts with you. Get to know yourself, understand your strengths and nurture them. Nobody is drawn to people who do not have direction. The majority of people like to be led, so if you cannot give them the right way to success, they will leave you. Understanding yourself makes it easy for you to find your calling, career, passions, leisure, profession and perhaps allow you to put all these together.

Lacking self-awareness is detrimental to your organization. Most if not all of your employees should be people with strengths that you do not have. Get to know your strengths and weaknesses in order to build effective team synergy.

Not so many people talk about emotional self-awareness. Business is packed with more failures than successes; therefore it is good to understand your emotional stability. Know how you react to both good and bad news because business brings both, and sometimes they can even come at the same time. It can be

85

overwhelming and even lead to health problems if you cannot cope with the stress that comes from leadership or starting your own business.

168 Hour Work Week

Entrepreneurs and leaders forget about a forty-hour work week. As a leader, you hold the potential of your organization and you can only be rewarded according to what you invest. More work, more reward, less work, less reward and that is how it is.

As the leader of an organization, be prepared to work until the wee hours of the night. It is also best to know your limits; do not push yourself too much, as this may lead to burnout. Most startup entrepreneurs are discouraged by looking at the amount of work that is required of them. The truth is, for good results, someone must get the work done, and since you are alone when you start a company, be ready to face it.

Having a weekly plan, as explained in earlier chapters, can help you to create a time slot for everything. Never forget to add time to relax, meditate and do daily devotions. "The fear of the LORD is the beginning of knowledge; fools despise wisdom and instruction" (Proverbs 1:7. ESV).

Even though you are striving for success, having a balance will draw you closer to God. Put smart work and faith together, for we cannot be fruitful if we forget the aspect of faith in everything that we do. Always remember to rest on the Sabbath. "Do not toil to acquire wealth; be discerning enough to desist. When your eyes light on it, it is gone, for suddenly it sprouts wing, flying like an eagle towards heaven" (Proverbs 23:4-5. ESV).

Focus

Leadership needs focus. I was once told by my grandfather of a person who wanted to be everything. He saw a hockey player dribble past the opposing team in style and make a spectacular score, and this gentleman said that he wanted to be a hockey player. He started practising, and after a few weeks he quit. A few weeks later, he heard a violin set piece played by Niccolo Paganini. He made up his mind to be one of the greatest violinists the world has ever produced. He bought a violin and started practicing, only to quit later on.

This same gentleman happened to have come across Leonardo da Vinci's famous *Mona Lisa*. He was perplexed at the beauty and artistic work that was put into the portrait. He then decided to pick painting as his next profession; after a few weeks, he quit. At the end of his life, he achieved nothing. This reminds me of a famous saying, "a rolling stone gathers no moss."

As an entrepreneur, you should focus on a single thing, do it to the best of your understanding, and if it does not work, then you can still point out to people that you did your best. In life, there are no failures, but there are projects that do not attain their founder's expectations. This does not make a leader a failure.

87

Martin Luther King, Jr. once said, "if a man is called to be a street sweeper, he should sweep streets even as a Michelangelo painted, or Beethoven composed music or Shakespeare wrote poetry. He should sweep streets so well that all the hosts of heaven and earth will pause to say, 'here lived a great street sweeper who did his job well,'". In everything you do, always do it well.

CHAPTER 19: CHARACTERISTICS OF SUCCESSFUL ENTREPRENEURS

"A business has to be involving, it has to be fun, and it has to exercise your creative instincts." ~ Richard Branson

"You were born to win, but to be a winner, you must plan to win, prepare to win, and expect to win." ~ Zig Zigler

"Whatever the mind of man can conceive and believe, it can achieve. Thoughts are things! And powerful things are those that, when mixed with definiteness of purpose, and burning desire, can be translated into riches." ~ Napoleon Hill

Fun

Your workplace should be a conducive to work in and successful entrepreneurs learn how to have fun despite the mundane tasks they are working on. Speaking from experience as the founder and executive director of an international Christian not-for-profit organization, drafting our organization bylaws and doing all the paper work has been the most boring part of my job so far. However, I looked at the end goal of why I was starting the organization and stayed focused on that single goal. For more than 3 months, I woke up, did research, wrote for almost the whole day and went to bed. As a music lover, I enjoyed my work more with R&B and acappella music in the background. If you love jazz, rock, metal, dance, dubstep, play it, and make your work environment a fun place to be.

89

Focus

This might sound rude, but nobody is going to remind you to be serious about the work you are doing. Take your work seriously and give it your best. When you get frustrated, and you will, then take a break and come back energized to give it another good shot. It is dependent upon you to perfect your pitch and idea before anybody else gives you a minute of their sweet time to listen to you. Once again, remember to focus and do it well.

Time Management

We are all given twenty-four hours in a day by God, whether you are Bill Gates or the "world's poorest president Jose Mujica," of Uruguay. Planning your time will take you far. Try not to have more than five items on your to-do list every day. Remember to get at least thirty minutes of exercise, because your body and brain work better if you are healthy.

Finance Management

This is a challenge to a myriad of entrepreneurs. You really do not earn a lot as a startup, so track your expenditure to the penny. A simple investment rule: never spend more than you earn. Remember, it takes a while before a startup can even pay simple bills such as a phone bill. Use your money wisely. I would also encourage you to give back to God what you think he deserves. I know many people give 10%, but I am not going to encourage or discourage you from giving. Just give what you think is fair to give back to God; it can be money, time, praise, prayer, discipleship, volunteering or many other resources.

Do it for Your Clients

Let me jump into my morality and ethics books and pull out one of the oldest tenets, "the Golden Rule." Put yourself into your customer's shoes; if you were the customer, do you think you would be satisfied with the goods or services that you are purchasing? If your answer is yes, then please continue in the same spirit. If your answer is no, then I don't think I have to tell you what to do. Always consider your customers first, even in background operations like accounting, promotion and designing.

Go for Nothing Less

My assumption now is that you already have your mission, vision and value statements written. Work with those, try some challenging things, pick up that phone and do a cold call, send that email to a customer asking them why they are not satisfied with your product, update your books, and if you are running a not-for-profit organization, ask that donor to support your project. Always challenge your guts and try something that gives you chills in your spine.

Get an Impeccable Business Team

Successful entrepreneurs never do it alone. They have mentors, business advisers, role models, partners, and they have a broad and healthy network of people who can share the often harsh reality of the markets they are in. If you are picking your own team, choose skilled and efficient members.

Create a Competitive Edge

What differentiates you from any other service provider out there? What is so unique in your product that I would forget about the already existing brands so that I can have your product on my table? This can range from the unique chemical composition of the product you are selling to the reasonable price. Always have a unique identity that puts you ahead of the game.

Educate Yourself

They say learning never stops. Reinvent yourself, learn new things, read those magazines, posters and newspapers, subscribe to blog posts, do research online, read books, sign up for seminars, take online courses. The list is endless. It is only when you admit that you do not know enough that you open more opportunities to become a stronger entrepreneur. Just do it!

Sleep

Most entrepreneurs and nerds are workaholics, get frustrated frequently and easily, are night owls, and may suffer from depression. Stop drinking that coffee late at night and give yourself a break. Relax, enjoy a good night's rest and wake up productive and ready to work as you've never worked before.

CHAPTER 20: UNCERTAINTY AND RISKS

$$\Delta \chi \Delta \rho \geq \frac{\hbar}{2}$$

Risk formula.

"Life is either a daring adventure or nothing at all."
~ Helen Keller

"A ship is always safe at the shore - but that is not what it is built for."
~ Albert Einstein

"Only those who play win. Only those who risk win. History favors risk-takers. Forgets the timid. Everything else is commentary."

~ Unknown

Risks are often discussed as though they are the only obstacles preventing people from getting to entrepreneurship, but what is really ment by "risks?" Is there anything else other than risks that can raise an entrepreneur's adrenaline? As an entrepreneur, if an action does not cause you to take a deep breath before you do it, then it might not be risky enough and that means that it is not as important.

It is also good to understand that there is no perfect risk out there. There is a lot of uncertainty with decisions we make, since we mortals can only operate in a linear time scale. In reality, people are not scared of risks but of the uncertainties that come with the entrepreneurial decisions you make. What are uncertainties?

Uncertainty refers to outcomes not contemplated during the decision-making process, while risks refer to outcomes that have been contemplated and are quantified as probabilities. The fact that risks are premeditated makes them expected and easier to deal with, but uncertainties are unanticipated occurrences, and those are the most dangerous ones.

Duo-contemplation is about how to respond to uncertainties. An entrepreneur needs to have clear thoughts when things do not go as planned. It can be draining to operate in such a situation, although uncertainties can also include unexpected positive results or unexpected successes.

Uncertainties can be a result of workers' skills not matching the required standards of performance, low productivity due to low employee morale or general mishaps and errors in forecasting. For this reason, entrepreneurs should give more weight to non-financial and qualitative factors than financial data. This is not to say that financial data are less important, but seeing past financial data can help businessmen to see their way to a comeback after adverse occurrences.

The duo-contemplation matrix covers recovery from both risks and uncertainties, and it heavily relies on the leader's ability to absorb market shocks and make wise decisions after a fall. For duo-contemplation to happen successfully, a leader should be ready for drastic changes. Employees should also be in a position to take the change with minimal or, even better, no resistance however before these changes happen, an entrepreneur or a leader should consider:

Emotional Effects

How are the changes going to affect the entire team that an entrepreneur is working with? Are they comfortable trying new things? If they are not, how can we transform their fears into cash flow-generating ideas? Business gurus succeed because they can answer these questions. Dismantling failure, and the uncertainties and fears that come with it, forms a strong base of success. As an entrepreneur, you do not want to be at the mercies of your emotions. Use your emotion to defeat itself. Transform your emotions into happiness and enjoy the outcome no matter what it is. Sharing this attitude with your employees builds confidence and a strong belief in the organization after drastic changes have happened. It is also important to know that any changes made should not be hard to adopt.

Psychological Effects

Let us take the mind as the organ of feeling, awareness and motivation. Anything that interferes with your state of mind negatively is what you do not want as an entrepreneur. This is not as simple as it may sound, especially after a failure. The idea of duo-contemplation is to have a strong and stable state of mind to help you fight all the

95

emotional effects that might come with a failure. The human mind is the most versatile organ in the body, and can be trained to respond positively to any action.

As devastating as failure can be, the human mind never runs out of tentative solutions to the main problems; there is no big challenge that the human mind cannot handle. "No temptation has overtaken you that is not common to man. God is faithful, and he will not let you be tempted beyond your ability, but with the temptation he will also provide the way of escape, that you may be able to endure it" (1 Corinthians 10:13). I wish every entrepreneur would read the Bible as it boosts one's faith when it comes to trying risky decisions. Based on this Bible verse, you can meet challenges of different kinds, but God has promised that you will not be overcome by temptations, therefore do not let your challenges affect your state of mind.

Why the Change

Entrepreneurs should not just propose a change because they feel like it is good to implement one. When making a change, plan and always remember to maintain your core values intact. Always have a positive and a better reason than before as to why you think a change is important. A change can be so big that it becomes insignificant. That is when change leads to permanent failure. Based on keen observation of the British Motor Works (BMW) X Series, starting from the X3 to the X6, there have been very slight changes at every stage, either to the chassis shape, gearbox setting, interior space, face lift or engine size. The changes are minimal, direct and relatively simple. They are identifiable changes that do not need extra work to learn or adapt to, especially from a consumer's perspective. The fact that you can also order a custom-designed BMW means that the changes suit your preference. The point: always have a reason why you are introducing a change and let it be easy to adopt.

How: The Art of Execution

Doing the same thing all the time, tremendous repeat or repeated abuse as one of my friends describes it is unhealthy. It is said that change is as good as a rest therefore change should be constant and always in motion. That is when you change the change. So how should people execute the art of change? Implementing the art of change can be hectic yet it can also be simplified through these key points.

- **The vision**: it is important to lay out a vision for what exactly is changing and how is it going to change. The vision gives a broader picture of what the team will work towards. This vision should be succinct and precise. By making the change vision clear, short and precise, you are simplifying it for your team to easily adopt increasing the chance that they will buy into it.
- **Specialization**: you want to match the tasks with skills required to accomplish them. Through specialization and division of labour, you are already simplifying the change making it easy to adopt. Clarity with each individual on how important their tasks and roles are to the vision of change helps develop a team synergy. Duo-contemplation works best if you match your team with what they can do best. It is all about maximizing the output from your team.

97

- ***Follow-up***: great leaders go to their employees to inquire if they are meeting any challenges. Try it, it works. You do not have to implement a change to do this. Just ask how you can help them meet their goals, make fun and create a lively work environment. How many entrepreneurs like to crack jokes with their juniors? You want to create an environment where your team enjoys your presence and the work they do. It is also important that you make them know that you are in control, a manager, a director, and the boss if you like calling yourself that.

Timespan it Takes to Change

How drastic are your changes? Are they changes that will take your organization ten years to adopt? Since you are working with startups and growing businesses, a change should not take your team more than three months to implement. It should be that simple. Design a change that impresses, a change that everybody wants to flock to. If you find it difficult to come up with one, especially after failure, then look at the reason why you failed or what you want to improve on and just tweak things a little bit.

Let us look at this example: you are a fruit vendor who sells a lot of bananas every week. In one week your sales went down due to bad weather and you are left with a lot of perishable inventory. Since you want to maximize your cash flow and revenue, you decide to have a banana cupcake business alongside your grocery to take care of the leftover fruits. This is an example of a change that does not require a long span of time to adopt. It is easy, almost obvious, and can still generate some income to support the business.

Realistic Goals

If you are a startup, you do not want to tell your employees or yourself that you are going to generate one billion in the first week of your business launch. Not that it is unfeasible, but setting realistic goals is always good. Start small then grow big. You do not want to risk a lot of your resources in a startup; losing it all is not good. Be economical; take it one step at a time and set achievable goals with a reasonable time limit. Most entrepreneurs are big dreamers; I am saying this out of experience. This can make it extremely difficult for your employees to match your expectations because you always want your books to read one hundred million dollars revenue in your first year. Give your employees enough time and realistic goals that they can attain. It is better that you give them short term and achievable goals that will grow your business than that you give them big dreams that they cannot achieve, making you close your business in the first few weeks it starts.

Planned Plans

When a king wants to conquer another kingdom, he meets with his military heads to plan and strategize the attack patterns. This is something that has existed through the ages: planning. You do not want to attack a giant with bare hands. Think of the Bible story in Joshua 18. Joshua sent out three representative to go and survey the land: they were to write a detailed description of what they saw and how to get into the land that they were promised. Joshua also lay

99

strategy on how to divide the land, who would settle in the South, who would go to the North and who would remain in the East.

A key lesson is, plan your movement. Plan your action. Plan and again plan the plan. It is really hard to win without a plan. That is why most politicians work with a campaign team. These are people who meet every day to lay strategies according to the location of campaign. Having been in African politics as a strategist to a member of parliament, I can say that strategists do more than what you see politicians say on screens or at a political rally.

After the speech, we analyze the clips word by word, gesture by gesture, information by information. We hold a quick meeting every day to update the candidate on what he did well and where he could improve. We also monitor his dressing cord and match it with the colours or symbols of a tribe or a particular group of people he is going to address. All this is planning, and if well executed it can result in a big success.

Uncertainty, risks and fear work like three horns of a triangle. Once you dismantle one side, the whole structure collapses.

CHAPTER 21: THE BUSINESS FALCONS

"Opportunity is missed by most people because it is dressed in overalls and looks like work." ~ Thomas Edison

"Take a lesson from the mosquito. She never waits for an opening, she makes one." ~ Kirk Kirkpatrick

"Failure is the opportunity to begin again more intelligently." ~ Henry Ford

"The pessimist sees difficulty in every opportunity. The optimist sees the opportunity in every difficulty." ~ Winston Churchill

Falcons are a species of birds commonly compared to hawks. Hawks are characterized by sharp talons, a large, curved beak and muscular legs. They use their sharp beaks to bite and tear their prey, and this makes them excellent hunters. Most entrepreneurs involuntarily act like falcons, hence the title "business falcons." So, in what ways are entrepreneurs like falcons?

Vision

Falcons have excellent eyesight; they can see up to eight times farther than humans. This helps with accuracy when spotting prey. They can identify the difference between a rock and a mouse when they are over one-hundred feet in the sky. Visionary leaders also see opportunities that lie miles away from them. That is what drives them to take action, either to bring about change or start something new. As an entrepreneur, always know what you are aiming for. Never pick stones when there is meat to be had. Be a falcon and reach for the best by zooming in on your target prey, and if it is worth the risk then dive in.

Spot Different Colors

Falcons have the ability to spot different colors. This is to give them precise judgment and accuracy when identifying prey. For correct judgment of potential prey, falcons must have a priori information on the different colors of objects that they see. The ability to distinguish profitable investments from fruitless ones is a critical feature of all business leaders. Entrepreneurs do not just see opportunities; they see opportunities with benefits. Like falcons, business leaders should be in a position to tell where there is greater potential for returns on all of their investments. You should be investing in colorful and lively places where you can get better profits, and therefore you must strategize before you take a leap.

Swiftness

After a hawk has calculated the distance and time it takes to catch their prey, they can travel at a speed of 200 miles per hour through the air to their target. This swiftness reduces the reaction time of the prey and creates a shocking impact when they land, making their prey dazed and confused. Once a business leader has seen an opportunity, it is up to him or her to act swiftly and take advantage of it before anybody else finds it. This is not to say that they should not allow competition; what I mean is that once you have your competitive edge, then always develop it to be ahead of everybody. Act swiftly and keep your rivals dazed at all times.

Be a Diurnal Leader

Falcons are always proactive during the daytime. Even though most entrepreneurs work late, it is advisable to work during the day and have enough rest during the nighttime. It is healthy and makes your brain work better and smarter. Avoid long nights, as they reduce your productivity. So stop filling that coffee cup late in the evening and have a restful evening. Catch up with family and friends, relax, and take notes.

Be an Opportunistic Feeder

What this means is that falcons can feed on anything they come across, from frogs and squirrels to insects and rats. They try to diversify their tastes in prey. Likewise, entrepreneurs should not narrow their views to only one type of product or service. Be adventurous, try new things. Mostly, your first ideas will not work, and that is why it is good to try more than one idea. Statistically, increasing your idea samples expands your probability of nailing the one that will succeed. Come up with one idea after another and keep improving them until you find the one that works. This can also be called fine-tuning.

As an entrepreneur and a not-for-profit director, I have tried more than eight business concepts, from farming to music production, and only three of the ideas that I launched have worked. I am still hopeful and adventurous, and I still work like a business falcon. If one idea fails, then I am certain that there is another idea out there that will succeed. If you are a startup, then my advice at this stage is to use as little capital as possible because you are still in the trial-and-error stage. You do not want to lose a lot on your first attempts unless you are certain that you are going to gain it back.

103

Joshua Okello

Always remember to play like a falcon.

CHAPTER 22: WHY BE A KING WHEN YOU CAN BE A GOD?

"Always dream and shoot higher than you know you can do. Do not bother just to be better than your contemporaries or predecessors. Try to be better than yourself."
~ William Faulkner

"You're alive, body. That means you have infinite potential. You can do anything, make anything, and dream anything. If you can change the world, the world will change. Potential. Once you're dead, it's gone. Over. You've made what you've made, dreamed your dream, written your name. You may be buried here, you may even walk. But that potential is finished."
~ Neil Gaiman, The Graveyard Book

"The potential of the average person is like a huge ocean un-sailed, a new continent unexplored, a world of possibilities waiting to be released and channeled toward some great good."
~ Brian Tracy

Styling yourself a god may sound controversial, but before you judge this chapter by reading the title, I would like to make it clear that I am a theist, who fully believes in Jesus Christ. Then what prompted me to talk of a god? The point I am putting across is that there is always a space for improvement and as an entrepreneur it is even better to go for nothing less than what you have set your mind on. Dream big!

105

Over the years, many kings were worshiped, adored and held higher ranks in their communities. In turn, some kings pledged allegiance to their gods, and in my view this gave gods prestige above all else. Let me reiterate that when I talk about gods I do not mean the divine God of heaven and earth, the maker of the universe and all that is in it. I am talking figuratively about holding higher rank in a business community. Is there anything that entrepreneurs can learn from this?

One of the greatest rappers of our time, Eminem, released a song referring himself as a "rap God." At the end of the song, Eminem asks, "why be a king when you can be God?"

As an entrepreneur, there is always room to grow into an *entrepreneur God*". You are more than you can imagine. Entrepreneurs are creative people who dream big, and as I always say, "go big or go bigger." Switching from being a king to being a God in the market place is the best way of flexing your entrepreneurial muscles over all your competitors.

As much as I do not believe in competition with business rivals, take what you do best and elevate it higher. To make a successful transition from being a king to being a god, an entrepreneur should have a grand plan or a blue print of his or her projects. Do your calculations and foresee your outcome before you implement them.

Most entrepreneurs start by drawing their goals, then working their way backwards to find the first step in their grand plan. Having a strategic plan will help you to develop a systematic approach of reaching your targets. Planning ahead of time reduces the need for improvising along the way, which can distract away from your goals. Always cause ripples, but never waste your time stopping unnecessary waves. What I mean is, come up with a step-by-step plan that covers all the challenges along the way and be ready to tackle them within the shortest period of time possible.

A friend of mine, a professor and a successful business consultant, has worked with goals, objectives, strategies and tactics (GOST) for his strategic plan. To be a God you must have a GOST. Goals are the immeasurable achievements that you want to attain in your organization, objectives are the measurable end products of why you are planning, strategies are what ought to be implemented to get your objectives right and lastly tactics are what you have to do to get the results you want.

You are in business because you want to be a God, so stop thinking like a king and act like a God. You are the only one who is standing in your way on the path to success. After all, why be a king when you can be a God?

Joshua Okello

_____

CHAPTER 23 IN THE BOXING-NESS RING

"You may encounter many defeats, but you must not be defeated. In fact, it may be necessary to encounter the defeats, so you can know who you are, what you can rise from, how you can still come out of it."
~ Maya Angelou

"Many of life's failures are people who did not realize how close they were to success when they gave up."
~ Thomas Edison

"I have walked that long road to freedom. I have tried not to falter; I have made missteps along the way. But I have discovered the secret that after climbing a great hill, one only finds that there are many more hills to climb. I have taken a moment here to rest, to steal a view of the glorious vista that surrounds me, to look back on the distance I have come. But I can only rest for a moment, for with freedom come responsibilities, and I dare not linger, for my long walk is not ended."
~ Nelson Mandela

It is time to fight! Your gloves are on, the ring is open, adrenaline rising, fear and panic can be felt, sweat drizzling. That is what it normally feels like in every fight. Now imagine you are in a boxing ring with an undefeated heavy weight, you are feather weight, it is your first time to fight, you do not know your opponent's skills and techniques, but you know that he has won ever since he started fighting. What do you do? That is what business is like.

Every boxer, whether experienced or not, feels the same way when they are about to fight, however, to win a battle, you must be armed with four fundamental things: fortitude, persistence, stratagems and endurance. Business should also be taken as a sport. The more you train, the more you familiarize yourself with the game. In boxing, it is always advisable to hit when you are least expected to, and as the rule of duo-contemplation suggests, if one style does not work, but an opportunity arises to adopt another acceptable style to win the game, then apply the alternative style. This rule keeps you from being shocked by any outcome.

Courage

As an entrepreneur, you are the leader. You must face your fears and knock them out before you can knock your opponent out. Remember the famous saying, "draw your friends close but your enemies closer." Get to know your fears very well and learn how to handle them. Be courageous when doing everything from responding to media questions to explaining your ideas to pitching your ideas. Some people will be convinced by your courage and how composed you are as you tell them about your product or service. Relax, and be composed and drive the fear away.

Every boxer knows the risks of fighting and the damage it causes to peoples' health, but that does not stop them from fighting. Courage makes them believe in themselves, and however many punches they get before they land a victory punch, they stay positive, knowing that they can do it. In business, you will face challenge after challenge and sometimes even close your business, but that should not make you quit. Go back to the drawing board and make a comeback.

Tenacity

November 9, 1996 was a big day in the world of heavyweight boxing. Evander Holyfield fought the great Mike Tyson in a game that saw Holyfield declared the winner. No one had ever thrown Mike Tyson or taken him to more than six rounds; unbelievably, Tyson lost in the eleventh round due to a technical knockout.

The two were real fighters, and held the fight until the very last minute. After rounds and rounds of exchanging blows, both were fatigued, but kept hope alive knowing that they could still make it. If you do not win by the scorecards in a boxing match, you still have a hope of winning through a technical knockout, which at this point was the best option for either of them. Even though Holyfield was ahead on the scorecard, the outcome of the match was still uncertain; most of Tyson's victories were won in clean knockouts.

Once you pick a business fight, fight it till the very last minute. Fight until you bring a trophy home. It is you who has to first believe in your product or service before anybody else does, therefore, if you quit, nobody is going to help you win the fight. Give your business your best shot, push it till the end. If you do not win on the scorecards, you can still win at the very last minute. Have faith, build it on hope and throw your punches until the very end.

Speed

In every game, speed is very important, but in boxing the match depends on it. How quick do you react involuntarily to a punch thrown at you? In what direction do you have to move? Which hand are you going to connect a jab with? And how fast can you throw a punch before your opponent blocks it? In business, you have to act on your feet. When you see an opportunity that can work, go for it. It is all about timing. Make winning seem effortless, but deep down your heart know that it took a good amount of work.

Strategy

Holyfield's strategy of winning the match was by keeping Tyson backing up. He was forcefully pushing his way to towards his opponent and attacking when Tyson least expected it. Fighting with a heavy weight like Tyson also requires a lot of patience. You do not want to take him down in the first round because there are chances that he will become tired out by the time it gets to the eighth or ninth round. Since he is used to knocking people out early, you want to keep him tired and then pull your best at last. That does not mean that you give him the opportunity to land easy punches on you. Every punch counts.

In business, strategy is the name of the game. Win through strategy, plan your moves and always create an exit plan when your original plan fails. Have a business plan and plan every stage of your projects. With a plan you have a GPS to success.

Go Past Your Limits

The only reason why boxers and other athletes hire coaches is to have someone to push them past their limits. That is what coaching is all about. When boxers are training, they lift weights, do push-ups, and all the strenuous exercises you can think of. They run, they punch punching bags, throw kicks and use any technique that can make them harder. They say whatever does not kill you always makes you stronger. Go past your limits.

Business is the same. What you put in is what you get back, therefore invest in your business, give it time and focus. Always aim for greater success, but avoid being greedy. Above all, enjoy what you are doing. Take business as a sport and have fun with it. The rewards are better if you succeed.

So pick those gloves and get ready for the fight. Go!

Joshua Okello

CHAPTER 24: SHARE YOUR THOUGHTS

"Either write something worth reading or do something worth writing." ~ Benjamin Franklin

"Writing is a form of therapy; sometimes I wonder how all those who do not write, compose or paint can manage to escape the madness, melancholia, the panic and fear which is inherent in a human situation." ~ Graham Greene

"I don't know how much longer I'll be around. I'll probably be writing when the Lord says, Maya, Maya Angelou, it's time.'" ~ Maya Angelou

As a leader and an entrepreneur, think of those who saw themselves as academics and scholars. They were judged by the content of their essays and magnum opuses. Some of them expressed arrogance in the highest degree, some of them had fine and well-formed ideas, some of them wrote responses that were well articulated, but all in all what they had in common was that they all shared their thoughts freely.

Thomas Malthus is crowned for his essay "The Principle of Population," René Descartes, is well known for his work *Meditations on First Philosophy*. Baruch Spinoza is renowned for his book *Magnum Opus, Ethica*. Plato for his writing *The Republic*, John Maynard Keynes, for *The General Theory of Employment*, Interest and Money. Machiavelli for *The Prince* and, of course, the writer of this piece for his book *Strategies of Entrepreneurial Leadership*. Great leaders or people with revolutionary thoughts always share them, either orally or through writing. As an entrepreneur, a pen and a paper should be your best friend.

115

Take at least two hours a week meditating. Through meditation you can develop new ideas, you leave your physical world and get into your inner soul. That is what meditation is all about. This is when you think of the unthinkable, imagine the unimaginable and visualize the invisible. Entrepreneurship radicalizes opinions that go beyond obeying the status-quo. The more people read your book, the more you are developing a cult-like following. As an entrepreneur and a leader, people should hold you close to their hearts; these are your die-hard fans who can defend you in your presence or in your absence.

Writing is another way of communicating, educating, marketing, and sharing your thoughts with the world. You might have the greatest of all the great ideas, but if you do not share them with anybody then they are the most useless things you own. I once was approached by a rapper who asked me what it takes to be great in the music industry, and so I asked him how many songs he had written. He told me that he had more than fifteen songs. My next question was, how do you share your music with your audience and he told me that he keeps his music on his phone. Really? Maybe he wanted people to listen to them through diffusion from his phone to their ears. Why are people afraid of sharing their thoughts?

Remember that the more criticism you get, the better you become in whatever you are doing. Share your thoughts with people, write, ask questions, and comment on other people's work. Who knows, maybe you will be the next Plato or René Descartes.

Business Plan

1. Business Summary.

- ❖ What is the name of your Business?
- ❖ What are the purposes of your business?
- ❖ How will the business be run?
- ❖ What value will it add to the society?
- ❖ How does it compare to competitors?
- ❖ What amount of capital do you need?

2. Business

- ❖ What is your vision statement
- ❖ What is your mission statement
- ❖ What are the business goals
- ❖ What is the history of the business
- ❖ What is the anticipated revenue and profitability?
- ❖ What is its expected cash flow?
- ❖ What is your greatest success?
- ❖ What is the competitive advantage?

3. Product

- ❖ What is the product or service you are offering?
- ❖ What is the greatest value it adds to customers?
- ❖ Describe its features, added advantage over other products in the market.
- ❖ Is your product or service a supplementary good or service?

4. Market

- ❖ Who do you anticipate to be your customer (Market niche).
- ❖ What is the demand in both short and long term?

5. Marketing Plan

- ❖ What are your marketing objectives?
  - Sales/revenues, diversification, growth, profitability.
- ❖ How are you going to test the market?

6. Product

- ❖ What is your product or service?

117

❖ Are you going to add or reduce your products or services?
❖ What is your strategy of introducing your product and services to your potential customers?

7. **Place**
    ❖ What is your geographical location you are going to cover?
    ❖ Why have you decided to go with this geographical location?
    ❖ How convenient and flexible is it to your customers?
    ❖ Have you factored in the transport costs and other operations required?

8. **Pricing**
    ❖ What is your pricing strategy?
    • Loss leadership strategy
    • Differentiation strategy
    • Penetration strategy
    • High End strategy
    • Scheming strategy

9. **Promotion**
    ❖ How are your customers going to be aware of your existence?
    ❖ How are you going to promote your product or service?
    • Advertising
    • Direct mails
    • Door to door
    • Leaflets and posters?
    • Word of mouth (Highly preferred).

10. **Management and governance.**
    ❖ Who is involved with the management?
    ❖ Who is in charge of governance?
    ❖ What are the skills and strengths required?
    ❖ How are you expecting to address challenges?

11. **Finance**
    ❖ Goal is to generate profit
    ❖ To have a steady cash flow to cater for bills and suppliers
    ❖ What is the business worth?
    ❖ Income statements (Profit & Loss)

❖ Balance sheet.
❖ Break Even Analysis: Break Event Point is the level of sales at which you start to exceed your costs – beyond this point, you start to earn profit.

12. What are the assets needed to run this business?

Joshua Okello

Index 1

Joshua Okello